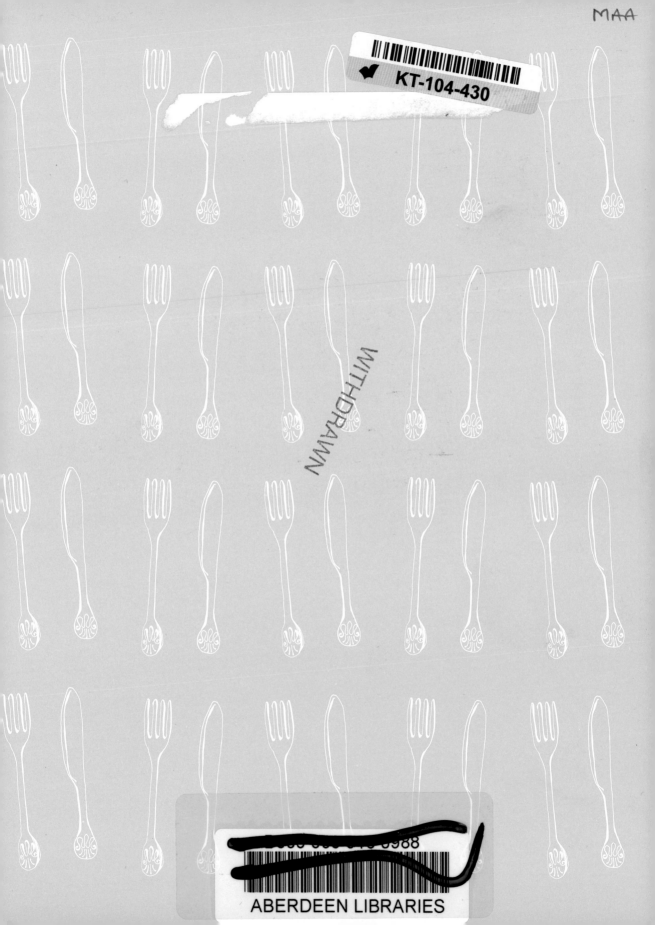

MAA

Sophie Thompson was the winner of *Celebrity MasterChef*, 2014. She is an Olivier Award-winning actress. Her films include *Harry Potter and the Deathly Hallows*, *Emma*, *Persuasion* and *Four Weddings and a Funeral*. On stage Sophie has appeared in many plays and musicals at the National Theatre, RSC and the West End. Television roles have included *The Detectorists* and *Eastenders*. She's been married to Richard Lumsden since 1995. They have two boys and live in North London.

'Sophie Thompson's cooking skills are the mirror to her acting. Deliciously delicate but painstakingly prepared, satisfying and uniquely blended, mouth-wateringly original. And her buns are a sensation!'
Derek Jacobi

'Sophie Thompson's cookbook is like Sophie Thompson. It's de-lightful, it's de-licious, it's de-lovely.'
Eileen Atkins

'Having been fed by the gorgeous Ms Thompson on several occasions, I can't wait to try out some of the recipes in this book.'
Denis Lawson

'Having supper with Soph is the most delicious affair. So many wonderful things appeared on the table, from homemade breads, hummus so moreish you could die (I didn't)!, and an array of dishes that were more than mouth-watering. They were divine. Think Olympus, think Goddess – that's my gorgeous friend Sophie T.'
Russell Grant

'Sophie makes it all so easy AND delicious.'
Alison Steadman

SOPHIE THOMPSON

My Family Kitchen

Favourite recipes from four generations

FABER & FABER

First published in the UK in 2015
by Faber & Faber Limited
Bloomsbury House, 74–77 Great Russell Street
London, WC1B 3DA

Printed in China

Publisher: Leah Thaxton
Commissioning Editor: Alice Swan
Editorial Assistant: Grace Gleave
Art Director: Emma Eldridge
Designer: Friederike Huber
Photographer: Al Richardson
Food Stylist: Frankie Unsworth
Recipe Testing: Bren Parkins-Knight
Props Stylist: Lydia Brun
Stylist: Katy McPhee

641.5

978-0-571-32417-0

2 4 6 8 10 9 7 5 3 1

for mum

into case & bake for 45" in slow
oven. Serve cold w. thin layer
of whipped cream decorated to.
walnut halves.

Coffee Mallow.

12 or so marshmallows.
melted in cup of hot Coffee.
Cool & when beginning to set
Stir in cup whipped cream. &
1/4 teasp. vanilla.

Mum's original 'Coffee Mallow Mousses' recipe.

Contents

Uncle James's tearooms

Granny Megsie and Grandpa Jacko

Publicity shot for *The Magic Roundabout* with Mum, Dad, Emma and I

Fridge cake on Walter's birthday

Eating lollipops with Emma in Scotland

Ernie's birthday

Granny Annie

Richard and I barbecuing

Mum

Introduction

When I was very small, about six I think, I decided I would invent a cake – create my very own recipe. I remember vividly that it was simply a mix of flour, sugar, currants and water (oh dear), which I baked until it was biscuit brown. It looked hard and rather unappealing, but I remained positive and offered it up. Dad immediately called it 'Sophie Cake' – that was my nickname for a long while.

Around the same time, Dad found me by the door of our larder rubbing malt vinegar on to my knees. 'What on earth are you doing, Soph?' he asked with genuine curiosity. 'Inventing an old wives' tale,' I replied, hoping that my knees would respond to the vinegar in some way that might prove useful. Another sort of recipe, I suppose. (I've just looked up the word recipe: 'a method laid down for achieving a desired end.' That makes sense!) Nothing happened to my knees, and Sophie Cake has not made it into this book, you might be relieved to know, but bit by bit, and mainly from the surrounding wonderful people in my life, I learnt to love cooking.

From Granny Annie I discovered thrift and faithfulness – mutton stew with barley. Rock cakes every Friday. Then there was Granny Megsie's inventive culinary cheekiness – she used to swill out near empty jars of jam into gravy, and always had a pan of quietly bubbling stock on the hob with something unexpected – like apple peelings – in it.

There was Uncle James's remote Scottish café, where I would help in the kitchen as a child, get to taste all the cakes (chocolate, pineapple, orange) and watch as the bubbles popped on his endless fragrant batches of pancakes. As my mum wrote in her book *How Many Camels Are There in Holland?*, 'He bought the tea-rooms in the village, lit fires, baked and got into the *Good Food Guide*. It was a golden era for us as we crammed into the cottage each holiday and became temporary staff, eating cakes and sweets and serving them, making pancakes, pouring tea and coaxing cows out from behind the counter.'

And then there's my amazing mum and her awesome artistry and ability to make our old kitchen table look like a scene from *A Christmas Carol* after Scrooge has decided to be nice.

For me, cooking has always been about sharing and spending time with pals and family, luring them in with tasty morsels so they'd want to stay all day. My favourite get-togethers are where the meal just takes forever, nobody feels that they have to clear up, and any children lurking can leave the table to play, and wander back for a leftover sausage or a spot of wobbly jelly.

It's not always Sundays, high days and holidays though, and having to cook every day for the family can be a challenge – the time, the money, the inspiration: all these elements can rob cooking of its larks. Sometimes your sediment sinks. Sometimes you need a shake-up.

I must confess doing *MasterChef* was a major shake-up for me. I found myself making food I wouldn't have dared attempt before. And now that experience sits on the shelf like a condiment, along with the salt and pepper, there to encourage me to be bold and try new things. With any luck, this book might help you try new things too, in which case, yippee.

I'm just a turn who's been on a cookery show, so the idea of me piping up about food, let alone writing a cookbook, seems faintly absurd. That said, I'm chuffed as an extremely chuffed thing to have got this opportunity to be able to share this bundle of some of my favourite recipes with you. They've been handed down, invented, begged and borrowed and ultimately made my own. I hope you'll enjoy making them your own, too.

Granny Annie's original recipe for ginger bread

Me behind the counter at Uncle James's café

Filming 'A Traveller in Time' for the BBC, aged 15

Filming 'Emma'

Performing in 'The Bacchae' at The Bristol Old Vic

Trying to look calm on *MasterChef*

Larder

& Spice Stash

Here's what I tend to keep stocked in mine:

HERBS AND SPICES

Allspice
Bay leaves
Bouillon powder
Cardamom pods
Cayenne pepper
Celery salt
Chilli flakes
Chilli powder
Cinnamon (ground and
   sticks)
Cloves (ground and whole)
Coriander seeds (ground and
   whole)
Cumin seeds (ground and
   whole)
Curry powder
Dried herbs, various (thyme,
   oregano, mixed)
Fenugreek seeds
Garam masala
Ground ginger
Mace
Nutmeg
Onion seeds
Paprika (smoked and sweet)
Red pepper flakes
Star anise
Sumac
Turmeric
Vanilla extract

PACKETS AND CANS

Anchovies
Baking powder
Bicarbonate of soda
Breadcrumbs

Chickpeas
Chocolate (milk, dark and
   white)
Chopped tomatoes
Coconut (milk, creamed and
   desiccated)
Cornflour
Dried fruits, various
   (apricots, raisins, golden
   raisins, currants,
   sultanas)
Flour (self-raising, plain and
   gluten-free)
Golden syrup
Lentils
Nuts, various (pine nuts;
   chestnuts – cooked,
   canned or vacuum-packed;
   cashews; pistachios;
   walnuts; almonds – ground
   and whole)
Polenta
Rice (basmati, aborio)
Rice noodles
Sesame seeds
Sugar (caster, demerara,
   icing, granulated,
   muscovado, palm)
Sunflower seeds
Treacle

**BOTTLES, JARS AND
   TUBES**

Balsamic vinegar
Fish sauce (nam pla)
Garlic paste
Honey (runny and set)

Horseradish sauce
Maple syrup
Mirin (Japanese rice wine)
Mustard (Dijon, wholegrain,
   English, dried)
Oils, various (olive, vegetable,
   peanut, sesame, truffle,
   walnut)
Peanut butter
Redcurrant jelly
Soya sauce
Sun-dried tomatoes in oil
Sun-dried tomato paste
Sweet chilli sauce
Tabasco
Tahini
Tamarind paste
Tomato ketchup
Tomato purée
Vinegars, various (red wine,
   white wine, rice, malt,
   balsamic glaze, aged
   balsamic vinegar)
V8 vegetable juice
Worcestershire sauce

FRESH

Eggs (free-range)
Garlic
Ginger
Herbs, various
Lemongrass
Lemons, limes and oranges
   in abundance
Olives, various
Onions/shallots
Tatties

Hot! **Soups**

3
2
1

bred
egg

Latis   cyoctr Ramen

medium choppe
2 cloves garl
Soften in J
tsp ginger pow
mb of fresh si
Soften
glass of c mmp

Soups, Starters & Morsels

My old mucker, Em, aka Lanky or Lanx because of her height, is a veggie. We met when I worked with her wonderful step-dad, Peter Copley, at The Bristol Old Vic theatre, many years ago in a production of *The Bacchae*. We were both playing in the chorus – the female followers of Dionysus, and our masks were half a bucket on a broom handle.

Peter kept saying to me, 'Ooh, Soph, you would love my daughter Emma,' and I remember thinking, 'Ooh crikey, I doubt it.' He kept saying to Emma, 'Ooh Em, you would love this girl I'm working with,' and she remembers thinking, 'Ooh crikey, I doubt it.' We met. He was right, and we've been friends ever since. She makes this soup. I love it.

Emma London's
Onion Soup
with Blue Cheese Toasts

Prepare in 30 mins · Cook in 65 mins · Serves 4–6

2 tbsp butter
1 tbsp olive oil
6 white onions, diced (a food processor will save time and tears here)
6 red onions, thinly sliced
3–4 garlic cloves
1 litre vegetable or chicken stock
1–2 tbsp dry sherry
1–2 tbsp balsamic vinegar
4 slices of good bread
butter, for spreading
120g blue cheese
salt and pepper

Heat the butter and oil in a large pan and add all the onions. Gently fry over a low heat for about 40 minutes until they are really soft and rich and almost caramelised.

Roughly chop the garlic cloves, reserving one for the toasts, and add to the pan; stir for a minute or two, then pour in the stock. Bring to a gentle simmer and then add the sherry and balsamic vinegar. Leave to simmer for about 20 minutes over a low heat. Taste and adjust the seasoning before ladling into serving bowls.

Meanwhile, toast your bread slices, rub with the cut side of the remaining garlic clove and spread with a little butter. Crumble over the blue cheese (you can substitute your favourite cheese, or use Gruyère for classic stringiness). Melt the toasts under a hot grill and float one on the top of each bowl of soup.

Hello gorgeous soupy thing.

I met my mate 'Spooky' Susie many years ago on a filming job up in Newcastle. All I can remember about the job was that it was something about a wedding and I had to be quite sad. It definitely wasn't *Four Weddings and a Funeral* – that was much later, and I had to be quite happy. (Just call me Vera Versatile.) Susie's husband Chris is a great souper and this is one of his. She is an amazing psychic and must have foretold I'd love it.

Chris & Susie's magic
Celeriac & Chestnut Soup

Prepare in 15 mins · Cook in 35 mins · Serves 4–5

generous knob of butter
1 tbsp vegetable oil
1 white onion, chopped
1 red onion, chopped
1 heaped tsp ground cinnamon
1 heaped tsp ground cumin
100ml dry sherry
1 heaped tsp vegetable bouillon powder
1 large celeriac, peeled and cut into chunks (don't be alarmed by its gnarly appearance)
800ml chicken stock
100ml double cream, plus extra for swirling
salt and pepper
100g vacuum-packed cooked chestnuts, crumbled and warmed gently in a dry frying pan
handful of fresh parsley leaves, chopped

Heat the butter and oil in a large pan, add all the onions and cook over a medium heat until softened, about 10 minutes.

Add the cinnamon and cumin and season with salt and pepper. Cook for a couple of minutes, enjoying that Christmassy aroma, and then add the sherry and bouillon powder. Let it bubble for a minute, then add the chopped celeriac and chicken stock. Bring to a simmer and leave to bubble away, uncovered, for 20 minutes, or until the celeriac has softened. Taste and adjust the seasoning.

Remove from the heat and use a stick blender to whizz the soup until smooth. Return the pan to the heat and stir in the cream.

Pour into bowls and add a swirl of cream on the top. Crumble over your warmed chestnuts and scatter with chopped parsley leaves.

This soup is dedicated to all the brilliant trainees at the Café from Crisis (a social enterprise set up by the charity Crisis to help homeless people receive training and get experience of working in a commercial kitchen). Especially Gavin, Fred and Angela. Not to mention Winston the Head Chef, who gave me the top tip to toast the cumin seeds. Thank you, Winston! I had a really great time there with them, making this heart-warming soup, in their heart-warming café.

I admit I'm not very fond of Halloween, but I do always carve a pumpkin because I'm very fond of *them*. One year I couldn't find one anywhere, except a beautiful blue-skinned one, so I discovered by accident how sweet the blue ones are. The colour of the blue skin and orange flesh is worth it just for how it looks. (No worries if you can't get hold of a blue one though – pick another pumpkin, or even a butternut squash, and adjust the seasoning to taste.) Pumpkins can be very hard to cut, so do wear your health and safety hat for this one.

Pumpkin Soup
with Cumin & Coconut
for the "Café from Crisis"

Prepare in 20 mins · Cook in 20 mins · Serves 4

2 tsp cumin seeds
1 tbsp olive oil
knob of butter
2 large shallots
1 medium pumpkin (about 1kg), peeled, deseeded and chopped into smallish chunks (if you are carving a pumpkin the hollowed-out flesh is perfect for this recipe)
300ml chicken stock
150ml coconut milk
salt and pepper

TO SERVE
sour cream or yogurt
chopped fresh chives, coriander
 or parsley →

Toast the cumin seeds in a dry frying pan until they start to release their aroma, then crush lightly with a pestle and mortar.

Heat the oil and butter in a large pan and add the chopped shallots. Cook over a low-medium heat until softened but not coloured, about 5 minutes.

Add the pumpkin pieces and stir for a couple of minutes, then add your crushed cumin seeds. Stir and soften together for a few minutes, then add the chicken stock and

about 200ml water, or enough to cover the pumpkin. Cook until soft, about 15 minutes, adding a splash more stock or water if needed.

Remove from the heat and liquidise the soup using a stick blender until nice and smooth. Stir in the coconut milk and season to taste.

Serve with a swirl of sour cream or yogurt and a scattering of chopped chives, coriander or parsley.

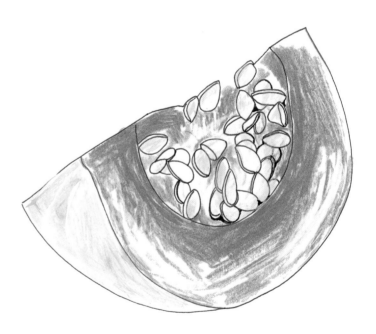

This is a recipe from my husband Richard's grandmother, Gwen Quirk (Great Gram). 'Gram' is not a typo. Our sons, Walter and Ernie, gave her this name when they were small and it stuck.

This soup is so warming and delicious and simple. A real Great Gram's special – she has made this for years (she is 97) – and the boys loved it from when they were tiny, which I have to confess I found surprising at the time. I thought they would be a tad appalled by soup... not Great Gram's.

The last time I made this I didn't have any chicken stock handy, but I did have some stock I had made from some bits of old veg in the fridge and a Parma ham end from Marvellous Maurizio, who runs our fab local deli, Amici. He told me that Italians often take the stubby end of the Parma ham and use it in their stocks. It really was so tasty. I love to have a pot on the go. My Granny Megsie always had one on her Raeburn. It makes the house smell cosy and you can use it in so many ways – I think of it as the compost of the kitchen.

Great Gram's
Corn & Curry Soup

Prepare in 10 mins · Cook in 25 mins · Serves 4

3 tomatoes
1 tbsp vegetable oil
knob of butter
1 onion, chopped
1 tbsp plain flour
2 tsp medium curry powder
2 tsp tomato purée
500ml hot chicken or vegetable stock
250ml whole milk
125g fresh or frozen sweetcorn kernels
salt and pepper

First skin the tomatoes. Score a cross through the skin of each tomato, place in a large bowl and cover with boiling water. Leave for a few minutes, then place in a bowl of cold water. Slip the skins off and then chop the tomatoes.

Heat the oil and butter in a large pan and sweat the onion for about 5 minutes. When soft and glistening add the flour, curry powder and tomato purée and cook, stirring, for a couple of minutes. Add the stock, milk, sweetcorn and chopped tomatoes and bring to a simmer. Cover and cook over a low heat for about 20 minutes.

Blend the soup until smoothish using a stick blender or in batches in a liquidiser. Season to taste.

I do love a good mushroom, and these are just such a treat of a starter – utterly toothsome and fragrant; I always feel it's a bit like eating a piece of forest floor... in a good way! You can play around with what you put in as well: favourite cheeses, a golden raisin or three, fresh herbs, a bit of crushed chestnut, some leftover risotto, grated Parmesan. It's all very possible, and all very easy and – most importantly – delicious.

Portobello Mushrooms
with Cheese & Pine nuts

Prepare in 10 mins · Cook in 10 mins · Serves 4

4 large portobello mushrooms
100g Gorgonzola
100g flavoured cream cheese (I like Black Pepper Boursin)
olive, chilli or sesame oil, for drizzling
2 tsp dried oregano
few pinches (one per mushroom) of chilli or red pepper flakes
1 tbsp pine nuts
4 handfuls of mixed salad leaves
salt and pepper
Duck Poo Dressing (see page 143), to serve

Peel the mushrooms and pull off the stems so you are left with four mushroom 'bowls'. Place these in a buttered oven dish. Preheat the grill to medium.

Mix together your cheeses and then fill each mushroom with the cheese mixture. Drizzle with whichever oil you choose (truffle oil, if you have it, is lovely) and scatter over the dried oregano. Season with salt and pepper (you won't need much salt, as Gorgonzola is quite salty). Sprinkle with a smattering of chilli or red pepper flakes and place your cheesy mushrooms under the grill until they are sizzling and soft, about 10 minutes.

Meanwhile, toast the pine nuts in a dry frying pan until golden. Arrange your salad leaves over four plates. Place a grilled mushroom in the middle and scatter over the toasted pine nuts. Dot with a little Duck Poo Dressing (see page 143) and serve.

My husband Richard has been going to Franco's, an Italian restaurant in Friern Barnet, for years, since he was taken there by his old mate Paul Mari, who is as good as Italian (his grandpa came over from Naples), but was born in Stoke Newington. Now it's on our first choice list for 'Celebration Meals'. Dan is front of house, and Martha is the cook. She is amazing and self-taught. She started there as a waitress when it was a little pizzeria and then she and Dan fell in love, and a restaurant was born (plus baby Frank).

Martha & Dan's
Delish Scallops

Prepare in 10 mins · Cook in 5 mins · Serves 4

8 scallops, with or without roe
1 tbsp olive oil
40g butter
250g assorted mixed mushrooms, wiped
    clean and torn
2 tbsp truffle oil
100g mixed baby salad leaves (I go for
    ruby chard for colour, lamb's lettuce and
    rocket)
black pepper

Pat the scallops dry on kitchen paper.

Place a large frying pan over a medium heat and add the olive oil and half the butter. When it melts and stops sizzling, add the scallops to the oily butter. Sear for 2–3 minutes on each side and then transfer to a plate and cover with foil to keep warm.

Add the remaining butter to the pan and then add your assorted mushrooms. Use whichever mushrooms you can get hold of – my preference is a mix of wild mushrooms as they have such a fecund flavour. Sauté over a high heat for a few minutes, then reduce the heat and add a good splash of truffle oil (about a tablespoon). Mix in until they are glisteny and soft and then return your scallops to the pan to warm through and get acquainted with the truffle mushroom mix.

Toss the salad leaves in a bit more truffle oil and then divide between four plates. Pile up a portion of mushrooms and two scallops on each one plate and finish with a grind of black pepper.

Raise a glass – cheers, Martha and Dan!

I am mad about prawns. My Granny Megsie, when she couldn't remember their name, once described them as, 'Those wee pink things that don't have waists.' One day, when I was lodging with my pal Otis in Kennington, I bought two pints of prawns to share with him. When I got home he wasn't there. I ate the lot and woke up in the night itching all over. I padded to the bathroom in the dark, switched on the light and behold... I WAS one of those pink things that don't have a waist. Luckily, my reaction was caused by greed and not an allergy, and I continue to enjoy prawns as often as I can.

Our youngest son, Walt, is also a prawn fanatic. We can hoover these up in a matter of seconds between us.

Walt's Lollipop Prawns

Prepare in 15 mins, plus marinating · Cook in 6 mins · Serves 4

1 tbsp runny honey
juice of ½ lime
1 tbsp light soya sauce
1 tbsp fish sauce
1 tbsp sweet chilli sauce
1 red chilli, deseeded and finely chopped
450g large raw peeled prawns, defrosted
   if frozen
2 tsp oil (sesame if you have it)
1 tbsp sesame seeds, toasted in a dry
   frying pan
handful of fresh coriander, chopped
lime wedges and sweet chilli sauce, to serve

Make a marinade by mixing together the honey, lime juice, soya sauce, fish sauce, sweet chilli sauce and chopped red chilli in a bowl.

Pat the prawns dry with kitchen paper and add to the marinade, turning to coat. Cover with cling film and leave for about 30 minutes.

When you are ready to cook, thread your prawns on to short skewers – I usually do 3 per skewer. Place a griddle or frying pan over a high heat and add the oil. Cook the prawn lollipops for about 3 minutes on each side, dribbling over the marinade as you cook them, until they go lovely and sticky. Arrange on a wooden board and scatter over the sesame seeds and chopped coriander. Serve with a wedge or two of lime, and some sweet chilli sauce.

I think it's worth investing in a food processor for these alone.
They are so simple and fragrant and my boys eat them like blinkin'
sweets. I love the fact that they are so utterly different from our English
versions of fishcakes. I think if I had to choose to eat another country's
food forever it might have to be Thailand's. These are lovely hot or cold,
so can be prepped for a bit of a 'do' long before any guests rock up.

Thai Fish Cakelets

Prepare in 30 mins · Cook in 20 mins · Serves 4–6 (makes about 16)

**1 stick of lemon grass, trimmed and roughly
   chopped**
2 garlic cloves, roughly chopped
**thumb-sized piece of fresh ginger, peeled
   and roughly chopped**
handful of fresh coriander
zest and juice of 1 lime
1 small red chilli, deseeded and chopped
1 small green chilli, deseeded and chopped
1 heaped tbsp desiccated coconut
½ red pepper, deseeded and chopped
3 kaffir lime leaves, fresh or dried
**400g skinless and boneless white fish fillet,
   e.g. cod, haddock, roughly chopped**
2 tsp vegetable oil
2 tsp toasted sesame oil
salt and pepper
**sweet chilli sauce, lime wedges, chopped
   spring onions and cucumber, to serve**

Put the lemon grass, garlic, ginger, coriander,
lime zest, half the lime juice, red and
green chillies, coconut, red pepper, kaffir
lime leaves and some seasoning in a food
processor and blitz until chopped really fine.
You may need to stop halfway through and
scrape down the sides of the bowl to make
sure it is well combined.

Add the chopped fish and pulse gently until
it is all mixed together (don't overdo it with
the fish, as you want the cakelets to have a
good texture). Transfer your lovely, fragrant
mixture to a bowl.

Rub the remaining lime juice over your
hands and start shaping blobs of the
mixture into little fishcakes. The mixture
can be quite sticky but the lime juice will
stop it sticking to your hands. You should
get about 14–16 fishcakes; place them on a
tray in a single layer and chill in the fridge
for at least 15 minutes to firm up.

You'll need to fry these in two batches,
so when you are ready to cook, heat half
of each oil in a large non-stick frying pan
over a medium heat. Cook the fishcakes for
about 4 minutes on each side, or until golden
on the outside and cooked through in the
middle. Try to avoid fiddling with them too
much while they are in the pan, as they are
quite fragile. Drain on kitchen paper and
serve on a lovely wooden board with some
sweet chilli dipping sauce, lime wedges.
Chopped spring onions and cucumber are
also a lovely addition.

I bumped into a bag of sumac one day in Tony's Continental in East Finchley (only the best greengrocer in the world). I was intrigued and at first I just sprinkled it on dishes of hummus. In this crab and avo cocktail I think it really pips the squeak and is the perfect 'secret ingredient'. I get my crab meat from my pal Pete the Fish at A. Scott & Son in East Finchley – it's lovely stuff.

Crab & Avocado Cocktail
with Secret Sumac

Prepare in 20 mins · Serves 8

FOR THE COCKTAIL MAYO
3 large egg yolks
200ml olive oil
2 tsp garlic paste (from a tube)
1 tsp Dijon mustard
1 tsp horseradish sauce
1 tsp honey
1 tsp white wine vinegar
4 tsp tomato ketchup
salt and pepper

600g white crab meat
3 ripe avocados, halved, stoned and flesh diced
2 baby gem lettuces, shredded
2 tsp walnut oil
2 tsp sumac, plus a little to garnish
1 lemon, cut into wedges

First make some cheeky cocktail mayo. Put the egg yolks in a large bowl with a generous pinch of salt. Whisk together with a large balloon whisk and then gradually start dripping in your olive oil, at first drop by drop and then drizzle by drizzle, whisking all the while until it thickens. This will take about 4–5 minutes. Then add the garlic paste, mustard, horseradish, honey, white wine vinegar, ketchup and mix well (add a tad more ketchup if you like your sauce pinker). Season with salt and pepper to taste. Cover and chill in the fridge until needed.

Put your crab meat in a sieve and press it well with a wooden spoon to squeeze out some of the liquid. Add to your mayonnaise along with the diced avocado and gently stir together. Let it sit and make friends while you arrange your lovely shredded baby gem in a bowl. Drizzle over a little walnut oil and a squeeze of lemon juice, just so your lettuce is glistening, then sprinkle generously with sumac.

To assemble: divide your lovely, nutty, lemony lettuce between your serving dishes – I love the look of this in cocktail glasses as it's a classic visually, but I find actually eating it is quite challenging as it is hard to mix and properly dig into without major spillage. So I serve mine on little dishes. Pile up a generous hillock of your crab and avocado mix and sprinkle with a tad more sumac, salt and pepper. Serve with a wedge of lemon, and maybe even a seaside song in your heart!

I do love a spot of mackerel. We catch it in Scotland, where we often spend our holidays. You can put out a special mackerel line and sometimes catch several at a time. We always throw the wee ones back. (I may seem calm writing this, but I'm SHRIEKING like a banshee when I have to take them off the hook.) It's such a beautiful fish and it makes me feel comforted and healthy when I eat it. If you happen to have caught some mackerel and you have a bucket barbecue and maybe even a beach nearby then I recommend filleting your fresh fish and cooking it straight away – just wrap it in foil with some lemon, butter and pepper.

However, if you're not on holiday near a beach with a bucket barby to hand, this is a top alternative, using smoked mackerel that's nice and easy to get hold of. No shrieking required.

Simple Mackerel Pâté Pots

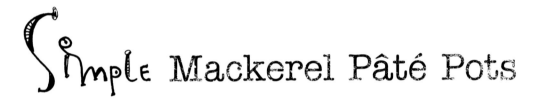

Prepare in 15 mins, plus chilling · Cook in 2 mins · Serves 4

250g smoked mackerel fillets, skinned
75g soft butter
2 spring onions, finely chopped
2 tsp horseradish sauce
zest of 1 lemon, plus the juice of ½
    (reserve a little zest to garnish)
50g melted butter
1 tbsp finely chopped chives or a few
    dill fronds
salt and pepper
lemon wedges and crusty bread, to serve

Flake the skinned mackerel into the bowl of your food processor, checking for any stray wee bones with your fingers. Add the butter, spring onions, horseradish, lemon zest and juice and blitz until combined. You can do this by hand but you'll need to mash the flakes of fish first with a fork before adding the rest of the ingredients. This method makes a rougher pâté. Season to taste.

Fill your ramekins and flatten the tops. Skim the froth off the top of your melted butter and very gently pour over the top of your ramekins, leaving the cloudy butter in the pan. Sprinkle with chopped chives or a dill frond and top with a little more lemon zest and some freshly ground black pepper. Chill until needed and serve with lovely crusty bread, or indeed your very own flatbreads (see page 38) and wedges of lemon. Add more pepper, if you are as mad for it as I am.

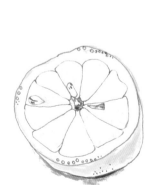

I first made this for my mate Chrissie, as she's particularly partial to a chicken liver. We met on a sitcom I did years ago for the BBC – Chrissie was the script supervisor. (She's a director now – a brilliant and liberally lauded one to boot.) We had a few too many cold beverages one night after work, and I remember her saying something along the lines of – 'I've never really been friends with an actor before, I've always found them rather unreliable.' I showed her – we've been friends for over twenty years. Plus she is godmother to the boys – that sitcom was a fecund job indeed, for I met a certain gent upon it, too – the father to the boys. Happy days.

This is one of those starters that always seems to get lapped up with glee – especially when served with homemade flatbreads (see page 38). It looks and smells so rustic and welcoming. There's something festive about a pâté too, I find, so it's a great way to start an epic meal at Christmas or on a birthday. It slows things down a treat, and the element of DIY as people have as much or as little as they want is very appealing.

Chrissie's Chicken Liver Pâté

Prepare in 15 mins · Cook in 15 mins · Serves 4–6

250g butter
600g chicken livers
1 tbsp olive oil
1 tbsp vegetable oil
2 large shallots, finely chopped
3 garlic cloves, chopped
3 large sage leaves, plus a few to garnish
175ml brandy
generous pinch of ground nutmeg or mace
salt and pepper
a few pink peppercorns, to decorate

First prepare your clarified butter. Put 100g of the butter in a small pan and melt gently over a low heat. As it melts, skim off the froth that appears on the surface and discard. You will then be able to see a clear layer of butter on top of a cloudy one. Carefully pour the clear fat into a bowl or jug and set aside, leaving the cloudy residue in the pan (discard this).

Prepare the chicken livers by cutting away any sinew and fat and cut each in half.

Heat the oils in a large frying pan and gently fry the shallots and garlic over a low heat until softened, about 7–8 minutes. Turn up the heat and add the chicken livers and sage leaves; cook for about 2 minutes until browned all over. Add the brandy and bubble for about 3 minutes, until the liquid has reduced down slightly. Set aside to cool for a few minutes.

Tip the shallot, liver and brandy mixture into a food processor and add the remaining 150g of butter. Season with salt and pepper and either nutmeg or mace and blend until smooth. Taste and adjust the seasoning and then spoon the pâté into a serving dish, or individual ramekins if you have them. Smooth the top of the pâté and garnish with a few pink peppercorns and a sage leaf or two. Pour the clarified butter over the top and chill in the fridge until set.

Serve with crusty bread or toasted flatbreads, pickles and salad leaves.

If you are not familiar with bresaola do try this wonderful Italian air-dried salted beef, cut thinly like Parma ham. I usually buy enough slices so that everyone can have four rolls each if they so desire, which they usually do as these are really moreish! Serve them on a big wooden board or a favourite plate so people can have as many or as few as they like. Most of my favourite big plates are from charity shops (ashets my ma calls them, think it's a Scottish word).

Bresaola Rolls

Prepare in 5 mins · Serves 4

16 slices of bresaola
handful of fresh basil leaves
125g ball of mozzarella, torn into pieces
4–6 sun-dried tomatoes in oil, drained
    and sliced
2 artichoke hearts in oil, drained
    and sliced
handful of pine nuts, toasted in a
    dry frying pan
olive oil, for drizzling
juice of ½ lemon
black pepper

Lay out your slices of bresaola and on each one put a basil leaf, a piece of beautiful, milky mozzarella, a slice of sun-dried tomato, a slice of artichoke, a few pine nuts and a drizzle of olive oil. Grind over some black pepper and then roll each one up, like a cigar. Transfer to your serving plate.

Once you have your plate full of fragrant bresaola rolls, drizzle with more olive oil and squeeze over the lemon juice. Add a smattering of pepper and scatter with any leftover pine nuts and a basil leaf or three.

A real quickie and great for gluten free'ers. These are lovely with soup
if you're looking for a change from regular bread, and they're
surprisingly delicious with a kipper. (I'm so very partial to a kipper.
My in-laws send them to us from the Isle Of Man –
thank you Anne and Ian and Roz the Postie.)

Corn Cheese &
Chilli Bread

Prepare in 5 mins · Cook in 20–25 mins · Makes about 16 pieces

200g polenta
200g rice flour
1 tbsp baking powder
2 tsp sea salt flakes
50g soft brown sugar
100g Cheddar, grated, plus extra for the top
 (optional)
1 tsp mild chilli powder or a pinch or 2 of
 chilli flakes (chilli flakes are hotter!)
284ml carton of buttermilk
4 tbsp olive oil
198g can sweetcorn, drained

Preheat the oven to 180°C/160°C fan/Gas 4
and liberally grease a 20cm square
baking tin.

Put the polenta, rice flour, baking powder,
salt, sugar, Cheddar and chilli powder or
flakes into a large mixing bowl and stir
together. Add the buttermilk, olive oil
and drained sweetcorn and stir until
well combined.

Pour the mixture into your prepared tin and
bake in the oven for 20–25 minutes until
golden. Remove from the oven and scatter
over a bit more grated Cheddar, if you
fancy, then place under a hot grill for 3–4
minutes until bubbly. Leave to cool in the
tin for a few minutes, then cut into squares.
Keeps for a day or 3 in tupperware, but best
served warmed through.

My Scottish Granny Megsie made two beautiful versions of toasted cheese. She always seemed to find a way to make the simplest things special. I remember when I was at college in Bristol and I'd give Megsie a call. There I was, getting up to all sorts of snoggy studenty shenanigans, and there was Megsie's voice on the line from a remote Scottish village, stirring marmalade and footling, and making me feel, despite all the delightful drama school frolics, that where *she* was, was clearly the place to be. The third version is my dad's absolute favourite Top Snack – what he used to call 'Fried Cheese'. I know. Sounds a bit wrong. I hope you will agree, once tried, it isn't.

Dad & Megsie's Toasted Cheese 3 Ways

Each version: Prepare in 2 mins · Cook in 2 mins · Serves 1

VERSION 1

slice of bread
50g strong Cheddar, grated
¼ eating apple, thinly sliced

Preheat the grill to high. Lightly toast your bread and cover with about half the grated Cheddar. Top with a layer of sliced apple, overlapping the slices. Add the rest of the cheese and pop under the grill until the cheese is melted and bubbling and the apple has softened.

VERSION 2

slice of bread
50g strong Cheddar, sliced
1 tsp marmalade

Preheat the grill to high. Lightly toast your bread and cover with oblongs of Cheddar. Grill until the cheese has melted, then spread the marmalade over the top. Return to the grill until bubbling.

VERSION 3

good handful or 3 of strong Cheddar, grated
Worcestershire sauce
hunk of good crusty bread
tomato wedges (optional)

Find a flameproof dish (I use a tin plate, which is tops for this) and scatter your grated Cheddar over the base. Place over a low heat and watch it melt and go bubbly – even a little bit burnt at the edges (the burnty aspect was paramount for Dad).

Dapple liberally with Worcestershire sauce, and eat with a hunk of bread. You will need a knife to scrape up the lovely brown bubbly cheese from the bottom and edges.

I must admit I love this with wedges of fresh tomato on the side. Dad would be appalled.

These sort-of-pittas are just the bees knees, as you can mess about with them depending on what you're in the mood for. I've been making them for years – since I was in college. Plus, they're simple and easy, and a bargain! I sometimes add turmeric just for colour alone. You can add thyme leaves or any herb, actually. I love loads of pepper in mine. (I'm a pepper addict.)

College Days
Homemade Flatbreads

Prepare in 10 mins · Cook in 25 mins · Makes about 12

**500g self-raising flour (I use gluten-free),
    plus extra for rolling**
2 tsp sea salt flakes
2 tsp baking powder
500g strained Greek yogurt

OPTIONAL EXTRAS
½–1 tsp ground turmeric
1 tsp fresh thyme leaves
½–1 tsp black pepper
etc!

Put all the ingredients in a large mixing bowl, adding whatever extras you have gone for, and mix together with your hands into a dough. Tip on to a lightly floured surface. You can make these breads whatever size you want – I usually go for quite small ones, flattening them out with my hands into little rounds (about as thick as a pound coin) as if I was making wee chapattis. You can also use a rolling pin.

Place a dry griddle pan (no oiling required) over a high heat and cook each flatbread for a couple of minutes on each side. They tend to puff up a bit and then subside. I do them until they have good griddle markings.

They just look gorgeous simply piled on to a big board. Delish with pâté, soup, hummus, cheese... So simple, easy, cheap and yum.

This is dedicated to my wildly talented sister, Emma, because she loves it even more than I do, and I sometimes make it especially for her on a Sunday – or any day when we endeavour to do family get-togethers. It's quite a different thing from the pink facepack variety, which I do have a soft spot for, I admit, but homemade definitely wins the taramasalata day. I remember being Mum's oil pourer-in-er when I was little. She didn't have a processor, so I would stand beside her, gently and very seriously dripping in the olive oil as she stirred.

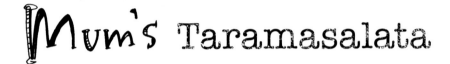 Mum's Taramasalata

Prepare in 15 mins · Serves 4–6 (makes 450g)

3 garlic cloves
350g smoked cod's roe
juice of 1 large lemon
100ml extra virgin olive oil
(use the best in your cupboard)
black pepper

Start by removing the little sprout or germ in the middle of each garlic clove. This germ sometimes has a rather pungent, almost bitter flavour, especially if your garlic is a little on the old side. This may seem a bit fiddly but as the garlic is used raw in this recipe, it's best to remove it to stop it overpowering the delicate flavour of the taramasalata. Simply slice each clove in half and use a small knife to pry the little green germ out. Finely chop the garlic.

Place the smoked cod's roe in a bowl and cover with boiling water. Set aside for about 15 minutes, or until the water is hand hot. Take out the roes and skin them.

Place the skinned roes in a food processor, add the garlic and lemon juice and blitz until smooth. With the motor still running, very slowly drizzle in the olive oil. Alternatively you can do this in a bowl with a wooden spoon and a strong, willing arm.

Taste and season with pepper (you won't need to add salt) and serve with crackers, crisps, bread or crudités.

There's never a time we don't have hummus in the fridge. In fact I think Richard, to whom I am wed, is half-man half-hummus. When I make it, I am overly generous with the garlic. I just love it like that, but I have had complaints! The version below is a less garlicky one in my book – literally.

Sunday Hummus

Prepare in 5 mins · Serves 8–10

2 x 400g cans chickpeas, rinsed and drained
4–6 garlic cloves (sometimes I add more...
   no wonder I've had complaints)
juice of 2 lemons
2–4 tbsp tahini (everyone has differing
   tastes as far as the chickpea/tahini ratio
   is concerned, so I tend to do it to taste)
approx 125–150ml extra virgin olive oil (use
   the best you've got)
salt and pepper
sumac, paprika, coriander leaves or pesto,
   to garnish

Put the drained chickpeas, garlic, lemon juice and tahini in a food processor and blitz. Keep whizzing as you gradually add the oil – the amount will depend on how smooth or grainy you like your hummus. Season to taste. If you don't have a food processor you can also do this with a stick blender. When I didn't have either of these I would mash the chickpeas with a fork. It's a coarser hummus (ooh matron), but it tastes just as good.

Garnish your hummus with a smattering of sumac or paprika or a few coriander leaves, or even a blob of pesto... crazy I know. Or just drizzle with more of your best olive oil and a grind of black pepper.

Everyone tends to have their own very particular version of this dip. For ages I didn't add chopped tomatoes as I felt that it made it too wet, until I realised I had to deseed them! It's so personal when it comes to the amount of chilli, too. When I make guacamole, it's quite spicy, but Richard's is always just right. The flatbreads (see page 38) are a corking friend for this, although the fellas in my house prefer the more traditional cheesy nachos.

Richard's Guacamole

Prepare in 5 mins · Serves 8

4 ripe avocados
½ red onion, finely chopped
generous dash of Tabasco
1 heaped tsp mayonnaise
1–2 tsp sweet chilli sauce
juice of ½ lime
celery salt, to taste (don't worry if you can't find celery salt, ordinary sea salt will be lovely)
black pepper
1 tomato, deseeded and finely chopped
a few fresh coriander leaves, to garnish

Halve and de-stone your avocados and scoop out the flesh into a bowl. Mash it good and proper with a fork and then stir in the chopped red onion. (Loving the colour combo...)

Add the Tabasco, mayonnaise, sweet chilli sauce, lime juice, celery salt and black pepper and stir together. Taste and adjust the seasoning. Finally fold in the chopped tomato. Garnish with a sprinkling of coriander – just a few fragrant leaves over the top.

I'm a bit mad about cheese. I'd rather have cheese than pudding any day, I confess. To drop a name, I did a film with the legendary Julie Andrews and she would always have cheese at teatime – she said it was the best pick-me-up when that afternoon slump occurred. Frankly, if it's good enough for Julie...

This is a great wee recipe of my mum's that uses up those curious cheese ends you are sometimes left with after a cheese board scenario. It turns those ends into a sort of cheese spread and is a lovely thing on crackers, or you can use it to make a flamboyant cheese on toast, or indeed a topping for a baked tattie.

'These are a few of my favourite things!'

(A special big thank you to my multi-talented brother-in-law, Greg, for the personalised cheese board.)

Ma's Devilled Cheese

Prepare in 2 mins · Cook in 10–15 mins · Serves 2

200g cheese scraps, grated or broken up (I last used some Gruyère, Taleggio, Cheddar and Provolone)
100ml double cream
1 tsp Dijon mustard
generous dash of Tabasco
2 tsp Worcestershire sauce
fresh parsley, to serve

Put all the ingredients into a heavy-based pan and place over a low-medium heat. Stir gently until it melts together but do not boil.

Pour into a couple of ramekins and cover with cling film – make sure the cling film is actually touching the cheese mixture to stop a skin forming. Chill in the fridge until the mixture has firmed up. Decorate with a sprig of parsley before serving.

'Climb every mountain!'

Richard's very partial to a pickled onion. His mum Anne makes big jars for Christmas every year. My gorgeous niece, Elbie, calls Richard 'Uncle Bridget'. Coincidentally, this is my pal Bridget's recipe, with some tampering Thompson tweaks. Dedicated to my dear brother-in-law, Andy, sister-in-law, Vicky, and little Elbs.

These onions in their jars make lovely Christmas gifts, and the cinnamon and star anise give them a special unexpected festive kick. But remember a pickled onion's not just for Christmas...

(Uncle) Bridget's
Pickled Onions

Prepare in 20 mins, plus overnight salting · Cook in 10 mins · Makes 2 large jars

900g pickling onions or small shallots, trimmed and peeled (cover with boiling water for a minute to make them easier to peel)
2 tbsp salt
568ml (1 bottle) distilled white malt vinegar
120g granulated sugar

FOR EACH JAR
1 small red chilli
1 small green chilli
6 whole allspice berries
small piece of cinnamon stick
1 star anise

Place the peeled pickling onions or shallots in a large bowl and stir in the salt. Cover and leave at room temperature for at least 12 hours or overnight.

Sterilise your jars. Preheat the oven to 140°C/120°C fan/Gas 1. Wash your jars thoroughly in hot soapy water and rinse well. Place the jars and lids directly on the oven shelf, upside down, and leave in the oven for 15 minutes.

Rinse the onions thoroughly in cold water, drain and pack into your sterilised jars. I like to leave the onions whole but you may find it easier to pack the onions in if you halve them. Add the flavourings to each jar so you can see them; the star anise, chillies and cinnamon sticks look so fetching.

Heat the vinegar and sugar in a pan over a medium heat, until the sugar dissolves and the mixture just starts to simmer. Leave to cool slightly before pouring over the onions. Seal and leave to pickle for at least 4 weeks before tucking in.

When we went to Scotland on holiday as kids, one of the first things we wanted to eat were tattie scones. Lots. They are the taste of my youth and they remain a tip-top favourite forever food. Simple. Comforting. Delicious. A bargain. An edible friend.

Tattie Scones

Prepare in 20 mins, plus chilling · Cook in 20 mins · Makes about 12

500g potatoes, peeled and cut into chunks
30g soft butter
1 tsp salt
1 large egg
150g plain flour
1 tsp baking powder

Cook the potatoes in a large pan of boiling water until soft. Drain and leave to steam dry in a colander. Mash the potatoes really well and allow to cool slightly.

Place the mash in a large bowl with the remaining ingredients and mix well to combine. Gather into a big potato dough ball, wrap in cling film and chill in the fridge for about 30 minutes.

Preheat the oven to 200°C/180°C fan/Gas 6 and lightly grease a baking sheet.

Roll the dough out on a floured surface – I usually do this in batches as I find it can be quite unwieldy if you do the whole lot at once. Don't roll the dough too thin; it should

be about the thickness of a pound coin plus a penny! Use a plate (approximately 20cm) as a template to cut circles of dough, re-rolling as necessary. Score each circle into quarters. Place on your prepared tray and bake on the top shelf of the oven for about 10 minutes on each side, or until pale golden in colour.

If you don't eat these all as soon as they are ready, you can store them in an airtight container. They are delicious hot or cold with...
lashings of butter
bacon and eggs
baked beans
scrambled eggs
mushrooms
anything you fancy.

I can't think of a nut I don't like. If Richard is half-man half-hummus, I am half-woman half-nut... I will regret writing that. As a child, cashews were my absolute favourites – the shape, the feel of them, the flavour – but I would be hard pressed to choose a favourite now. I'm just a nut fan. These are really first-rate as a crunchy pal to the olive if you are indulging in a few top beverages and are in need of an accompanying snack. Or just scoff them while watching the box with a cuppa soup.

Prepare in 5 mins · Cook in 6–8 mins · Makes 600g

200g raw almonds
200g raw hazelnuts
200g cashews
4 tsp runny honey
3 tsp cumin seeds, lightly crushed
2 tsp ground coriander
2 tsp red pepper flakes
2 tsp celery salt
2 tsp dried mixed herbs

Preheat the oven to 200°C/180°C fan/Gas 6.

Tip the almonds on to a baking tray and roast in the oven for about 8 minutes, just until they brown a bit and are starting to sweat their oils. Keep an eye on them and 'shoogle' them a couple of times during cooking so they roast evenly. Turn out into a bowl.

Repeat with the hazelnuts and then the cashews and add to the bowl of almonds.

(The cashews will roast more quickly, so keep an even beadier eye on them.)

Meanwhile melt the honey in a wok. Remove from the heat, add all the nuts and stir through. Add all the remaining ingredients and then have a 'beachy' moment by using your hands to work the herbs, spices and honey all over the nuts, as if you were playing with pebbles.

Spread out on a tray to cool and dry. Store in an airtight container somewhere dry and dark – if you haven't eaten them all before the weekend is out.

Dry martini anyone?

Note: Don't worry if they clump together a bit while being stored – they'll break up again easily. The slight stickiness is all part of their nutty charm.

chorizo
prawns
(mussels)

I found this recipe on my mum's recipe shelf, typed out and splattered on. She's never served it up to me though, which I'm rather put out about, as it's really delicious. I liked the look of it, as it seemed a bit different but not too complicated, and a great one for making good use of a whole bunch of your aromatic spices. It's also a good one to prepare in advance, as the fish balls benefit from an overnight stay in the fridge, plus spicey sauces always bloom, given some time... That said, I have made and eaten it the same day, and it was a bit of all right, if I say so myself! If making the koftas is a little too time-consuming for you, this recipe would be equally good with whole fillets of fish poached in the sauce.

fi^osh Kofta Curry

Prepare in 30 mins, plus cooling · Cook in 1 hour · Serves 4

FOR THE KOFTAS
1 tbsp olive oil, plus extra for frying
450–500g mixed skinned fish,
   such as cod, haddock and salmon,
   cut into bite-sized pieces
½ onion, grated
1 large egg, beaten
1–2 garlic cloves
1 tsp ground ginger
1 tsp ground cumin
1 tsp garam masala
½ tsp mild chilli powder
salt and pepper

FOR THE SAUCE
2 tbsp olive or vegetable oil
1 onion, finely chopped
6 cardamom pods, lightly crushed with
   a pestle and mortar
6 whole cloves

1 cinnamon stick
1 tsp ground turmeric
1 tsp cumin seeds, lightly crushed
1 tsp ground coriander
½ tsp mild chilli powder (more if you
   like it hot)
2 tsp black onion seeds
½ tsp fenugreek seeds
2 dried bay leaves
2 potatoes, peeled and chopped
1 apple, peeled, cored and chopped
1 tsp runny honey
4 tomatoes, chopped
300ml fish stock
150ml coconut cream
chopped fresh coriander, to garnish →

To make the koftas, heat the oil in a large, non-stick frying pan and add the fish. Fry for 4–5 minutes, turning carefully. Remove from the pan and allow to cool.

Squeeze the grated onion to remove any excess juice and then put in a large bowl along with the remaining kofta ingredients. When the fish is cool enough to handle, flake with your fingers, feeling for any stray bones, and then add to the bowl. Mix well and season with salt and pepper, then squeeze into 12 small balls. Cover loosely with cling film and chill in the fridge for at least 1 hour to firm up.

Meanwhile make the sauce. Heat the oil in a wok or deep frying pan over a medium heat and add the onion. Cook for 10 minutes, stirring occasionally. Add all the spices (whole and ground) and cook for 2 minutes, stirring continuously. Add the potatoes, apple, honey and tomatoes and stir together for a few minutes before adding the stock and coconut cream. Bring to the boil, then reduce the heat, cover and simmer for 30 minutes, until the potatoes are cooked through.

Shallow fry your chilled fish balls in batches; heat a little oil in a frying pan and brown them on all sides. Don't move them about too much in the pan; they have a more delicate constitution than your average meatball. Remove from the pan with a slotted spoon and drain on kitchen paper.

When you are nearly ready to eat, add the kofta balls to the pan, easing them into the gently simmering sauce. Cover the pan and poach for 10 minutes. Serve with a scattering of coriander leaves.

I do love a good fishcake, but so often I find that they're just
not quite fishy enough – that fish-to-potato ratio can be a stumbler…
I do hope you find this version fishy enough
and I don't get angry letters.

Salmon & Dill
Fishcakes

Prepare in 20 mins, plus cooling and chilling · Cook in 55 mins · Makes 10–12

**600g Desiree potatoes, peeled and cut into
  chunks**
3–4 tbsp vegetable oil
400g skinned salmon fillet (in one piece)
200g smoked salmon, chopped
1 tsp mustard powder
1 tsp horseradish sauce
zest of 1 lemon
small bunch of dill, fronds chopped
1 large egg, beaten
60g fresh breadcrumbs
½ tsp celery salt
salt and pepper
lemon slices, to serve

Cook the potatoes in a large pan of boiling
salted water until soft but not completely
falling apart (about 20 minutes). Drain and
leave to steam dry in the colander. Mash
well, using a potato ricer if you have one.
Set aside.

Heat 1 tablespoon of oil in a large frying pan
and cook the salmon fillet over a medium
heat for about 5 minutes each side. Transfer
to a plate to cool.

Flake the cooled salmon into a large bowl,
feeling for any stray bones as you go. Add
the mashed potato, smoked salmon, mustard
powder, horseradish, lemon zest and beaten
egg. Add most of the dill, saving a few
fronds for garnishing at the end. Season
with salt and pepper and then mix really
well with your hands. Cover with cling film
and chill in the fridge for at least 1 hour.

When ready to cook, preheat the oven to
200°C/180°C fan/Gas 6. Drizzle a tablespoon
of oil over the base of a large baking tray.

Mix together the breadcrumbs and celery
salt in a shallow dish. Shape the chilled
mixture into patties – you should get
between 10 and 12 fishcakes. Press
lightly into the breadcrumbs to coat all
over and place on the baking tray. Drizzle
the tops of the fishcakes with a little
more oil and then bake in the oven for
approximately 25 minutes, turning halfway
through cooking. The fishcakes can also be
pan-fried in a few tablespoons of oil over a
medium heat; they'll need about 6 minutes
on each side.

Sprinkle over your remaining dill and serve
with the lemon slices.

This is inspired by a fish stew that I shared with my beautiful pal Tam, in her restaurant, the Hampshire Hog. Making this was the first time I had ever made a fish stock. It's brilliant and easy. Your fishmonger will happily hand over his bits – ooh matron. I'm lucky to have Pete, our wonderful fishmonger, near where we live and he'll order anything in – what could be more fantastic? Let's hear it for independent shops!

Tam's Fish Stew

Prepare in 20 mins · Cook in 1 hour 40 mins · Serves 6–8

FOR THE STOCK
1 tbsp vegetable oil
2 carrots, roughly chopped
2 onions, roughly chopped
1 fennel bulb, chopped
1.5kg mixed fish bones and heads, rinsed well (not from oily fish – it can make a rather fatty and strong-smelling stock)
2 tbsp tomato purée
100ml Pernod
150ml dry white wine

FOR THE STEW
1 tbsp vegetable oil
1 red onion, finely sliced
4 spring onions, chopped
1 fennel bulb, halved and thinly sliced
1 red chilli, deseeded and chopped
16 new potatoes
100ml Pernod
12 cherry tomatoes, halved
400g prepared squid, cut into rectangles and scored
500g skinless cod or haddock, chopped
salt and pepper
dill leaves, to garnish
crusty garlic bread, to serve

First of all, make your fish stock. Heat the oil in a large pan and add the carrots, onions and fennel. Cook gently for 5 minutes, stirring occasionally. Add the fish bones and heads and cook for a further 10 minutes, until the remnants of fish on the bones look cooked. Add the tomato purée, Pernod and white wine and cook gently for 10 minutes. Add 1.5 litres of cold water and bring to a simmer. Continue to simmer over a medium heat for a good 40 minutes.

Meanwhile, start on the stew base. Heat the oil in a large pan and add the red onion, spring onions, fennel and chilli. Cook for 15 minutes, stirring occasionally. Set aside.

Cook the new potatoes in a pan of boiling salted water for 15–20 minutes, or until tender. Drain and halve them and set aside.

When your stock has done its simmering, strain it so you are left with your lovely orange red liquor. Return the strained stock to the pan (discard the bones and vegetables) and reduce over a high heat for about 20 minutes, or until you have about 500ml of liquid.

Add the reduced stock to the cooked onions, fennel and chilli. Add the Pernod and cook gently for 5 minutes. Add the halved potatoes, cherry tomatoes, squid and fish and cook for 10 minutes, stirring gently. Check that the fish is cooked through. Taste and adjust the seasoning.

Garnish with dill and serve in big bowls with crusty garlic bread.

Note: If you have some raw peeled prawns to hand – as you do – there's nothing to stop you adding a handful with the rest of the fish.

Whenever I say I'm going to cook a fish dish, Richard always suggests I do this one. It was the first fish recipe I think I ever made him, and it's stuck as his fave, even though I've made loads more since. He is particularly partial to the roasted cauliflower I serve alongside it.

Richard's Favourite Baked Fish

Prepare in 20 mins · Cook in 1 hour 5 mins · Serves 4

FOR THE SAUCE
500g good-quality ripe tomatoes
4 tbsp vegetable oil
1 onion, chopped
2 garlic cloves, finely chopped
1 tsp muscovado sugar
20g butter
200g wild mushrooms (or a mixture of wild and chestnut), wiped and sliced
25g bunch of basil, leaves torn
1 tbsp capers, chopped
salt and pepper

FOR THE ROASTED CAULIFLOWER
1kg cauliflower, cut into florets
2 tbsp olive oil
1 tsp cumin seeds, lightly crushed
2 tsp sesame seeds

600g skinless white fish fillet, such as cod loin or haddock, cut into 4 portions
40g black olives, stoned and chopped
juice of ½ a lemon

Preheat the oven to 180°C/160°C fan/Gas 4.

First make the tomato sauce. Score a cross through the skin of each tomato, place in a large bowl and cover with boiling water. Leave for a few minutes, then place in a bowl of cold water. Slip the skins off and chop the tomatoes.

Heat half the oil in a large pan and add the onions and garlic. Cook for about 10 minutes over a low-medium heat, stirring occasionally. Add the chopped tomatoes, sugar and seasoning and cook for a further 10 minutes, until thick and reduced. Meanwhile, melt the butter and remaining oil in a frying pan and add the mushrooms. Cook over a high heat for about 5 minutes, until golden. Add to the tomato sauce and continue to cook for 15 minutes. Season to taste and stir in the torn basil leaves and capers.

Meanwhile, place the cauliflower florets in a roasting tin and drizzle over the olive oil. Scatter over the bruised cumin seeds and seasoning and bake in the oven for 30 minutes, until tender and a little charred at the edges.

Place the fish fillets in an ovenproof dish and sprinkle over the chopped olives, lemon juice and salt and pepper. Spoon the sauce over the top, cover with foil and bake in the oven for about 20–25 minutes.

Just before serving, toast the sesame seeds in a dry frying pan until oily and golden (it takes just seconds, so shake the pan so that they don't burn). Sprinkle over the cauliflower and serve alongside the fish and tomato sauce.

Salmon is, I think, the first fish I ever tried. Even when I was very small I loved it in a sandwich. We used to go to the Player's Theatre in Villiers Street up West, to see my mum's cousin 'Auntie' Eleanor in various shows. She had the most amazingly powerful singing voice and stage presence, and I would sit there with my little legs sticking straight out, a glass of pop and a smoked salmon sarny in my hands, in utter happiness.

Dad used to go salmon fishing in Scotland and would get his catches oak-smoked on the Isle of Bute. This is a lovely rich recipe using – let's face it – two of Scotland's finest ingredients, salmon and whisky – hello! For a Friday night treat 'Him Indoors' likes this with chip shop chips, but it works with almost any veg too, like green beans – the other night I served it with roasted cauliflower (see page 59) and some peas roughly mashed with a bit of green pesto.

Salmon Steaks
with Scotch Whisky
& Brown Shrimp Sauce

Prepare in 15 mins · Cook in 15 mins · Serves 4

½ lemon
4 x 125g skinless and boneless salmon fillets
4 large slices smoked salmon
generous knob of butter, softened
salt and pepper

FOR THE SAUCE
2 tsp butter
3 tsp plain flour
4 tbsp whisky
200ml crème fraîche
2 tsp horseradish sauce
a generous squeeze of lemon juice
100g peeled brown shrimp
few dill sprigs

Preheat the oven to 180°C/160°C fan/Gas 4.

Cut three slices from the lemon and then cut each slice into quarters. Lightly season each salmon fillet and wrap with a slice of smoked salmon. Dot three dots of butter over the top of each fillet and place a quarter slice of lemon on each. Place each salmon fillet on a square of greaseproof paper and wrap loosely, scrunching up the ends so that it is in its own wee parcel. Place on an oven tray and bake in the oven for 15 minutes.

Meanwhile make the sauce. Melt the butter in a pan, add the flour and cook, stirring, for 1–2 minutes. Add the whisky and keep stirring over a very low heat so no lumps form. Add the crème fraîche, horseradish and lemon juice (to taste) and stir well until you have a smooth sauce. Add the shrimp and season to taste. If it needs thinning, add a little more wonderful warming whisky.

Just before serving, stir a few dill sprigs into the sauce. Unwrap the salmon parcels and serve with the sauce spooned over.

We have the best neighbours, Anu and Steve and their adorable boys Loki, Arun and Raul. Anu shared this quick fish curry recipe with me and I love it. It really is quick – she doesn't lie (she's a lawyer...) and so delish.

Anu & Steve's
Quick Fish Curry

Prepare in 20 mins · Cook in 45 mins · Serves 4

FOR THE CURRY
1 tbsp vegetable oil
1 tbsp olive oil
1 red onion, chopped
1 white onion, chopped
2 garlic cloves, thinly sliced
thumb-sized piece of fresh ginger,
    peeled and grated
½ tsp ground turmeric
½ tsp garam masala
½ tsp mild chilli powder
½ tsp ground cumin
½ tsp ground coriander
½ tsp salt
2 large tomatoes, chopped
150g green beans chopped
400ml can coconut milk
250–300g skinned salmon, cut into chunks
250–300g skinned haddock, cut into chunks
225g large peeled prawns, defrosted
    if frozen

FOR THE POTATOES
1kg potatoes, peeled and thickly sliced
1 tbsp olive oil
2 tsp black onion seeds
1 tsp lemon salt

Preheat the oven to 220°C/200°C fan/Gas 7.

For the potatoes, mix the sliced potatoes in a large bowl with the olive oil, black onion seeds and lemon salt. (If you can't find lemon salt, use sea salt mixed with some grated lemon zest.) Tip into a large roasting tin and cook in the oven for 30–35 minutes, turning once.

Heat both oils in a deep, wide lidded sauté pan over a medium heat. Add the onions and cook for 10 minutes, until lightly golden. Add the garlic and ginger and cook for a minute. Then add all the dried spices and salt and cook, stirring, for 2 minutes. Add the chopped tomatoes and chopped green beans. Cook for a few minutes before adding the coconut milk. Bring to a gentle simmer and then cook the sauce for about 5 minutes, to allow the flavours to develop. Taste and adjust the seasoning.

Add all the fish and prawns to the sauce, gently pushing the pieces under the liquid. Cover with a lid and leave to simmer gently for 8–10 minutes. Check that the fish is cooked through and then turn off the heat and leave to stand for a few minutes.

Serve straight from the pot with the fabulous roasted potato slices.

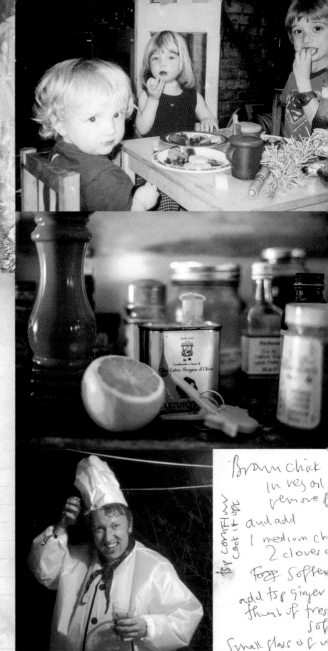

Orange Chicken

Chicken pieces
1 cup fresh orange juice
1 teaspoon ground ginger
1 clove garlic pressed.
1 piece onion
½ teaspoon salt, ¼ teaspoon pepper

Cut chicken into 6 or 8 portions & put in buttered casserole.

For the first 20 minutes cook with casserole closed.

Then pour over the sauce, take the lid off casserole & keep on basting until chicken is brown & tender

Cook in oven at 350
about 1 hour

Brown chick
in veg oil
remove
and add
1 medium ch
2 cloves
soften
add tsp ginger
thumb of fres
sof
small glass of w

by MARGARET STEVENSON

MEET THE MAGIC ROUNDABOUT MAN

This was inspired by a much simpler recipe of my Granny Annie's that I came across. I wish she was still around so I could serve it up to her. I'd have to keep quiet about the wine though. She used to watch Mum pouring the wine dregs into whatever she was cooking and mutter, 'Ooh Philly,' with a mixture of disapproval and awe.

Orange & Ginger Chicken

Prepare in 15 mins · Cook in 1½ hours · Serves 4

FOR THE CHICKEN
1 tbsp vegetable oil
1 tbsp butter
1.8–2kg whole chicken, jointed (if you have a friendly butcher, ask him to do it for you)
1 onion, finely chopped
2 garlic cloves, finely chopped
1 tsp ground ginger
1 heaped tbsp finely grated fresh ginger
240ml dry white wine
400ml freshly squeezed orange juice
2 tsp cornflour
salt and pepper

FOR THE RICE
small bunch of fresh coriander
juice of ½ lemon
2 tbsp olive oil
250g rice
2 tsp sesame oil
a generous pinch of sea salt

Preheat the oven to 180°C/160°C fan/Gas 4.

Heat the oil and butter in a large deep sauté pan over a medium-high heat. Add the chicken pieces and brown all over for about 4–5 minutes, then transfer to a large lidded casserole dish.

Add the onion and garlic to the sauté pan, reduce the heat and cook for about 5 minutes in the chicken-y butter and oil, or until softened. Add the ground and fresh ginger and cook for 2 minutes. Add the wine and bubble vigorously for 30 seconds, then add the orange juice and stir well.

Mix the cornflour in a cup with 2 tablespoons of the liquid from the pan. Stir well and then return to the pan. Let it bubble for a couple of minutes until you have a lovely orangey sauce, season, add some orange zest and then pour over the chicken pieces. Cover with a lid and cook in the oven for 45 minutes. Then cook for a further 30 minutes with the lid off.

While the chicken is cooking, prepare the rice. Blitz the coriander, lemon juice and 1 tablespoon of olive oil in a mini food processor, if you have one. Alternatively just chop the coriander very finely by hand and then stir into the lemon juice and oil. Bring a large pan of salted water to the boil and add the remaining olive oil and a squeeze of lemon juice. Add the rice and cook until just tender. Drain and then mix with the sesame oil, salt and coriander mixture for a beautiful bright green colour.

I like to press the rice into small ramekins or moulds and then turn out on to each plate. Serve with the wonderfully orangey, gingery chicken.

This is so quick and full of veggie, fishy, meaty goodness. Also, it's a whole meal in one pan... what's not to love? If you don't have chorizo, just use a bit of regular salami. If you don't have any of the meats, just use the fish and vice versa. You can just do your thing. Obviously if you have had a chance to get hold of all these ingredients, it's well worth it.

Speedy Supper Paella

Prepare in 20 mins · Cook in 40 mins · Serves 4

1 tbsp vegetable oil
1 tbsp chilli oil
1 onion, thinly sliced
2 skinless chicken breast fillets (about 175g each), chopped into bite-sized pieces
1-2 tsp sweet smoked paprika
3 garlic cloves, finely chopped
150g piece of chorizo, peeled and chopped
1 small red pepper, deseeded and sliced
1 small yellow pepper, deseeded and sliced
300g paella or risotto rice
300ml dry white wine
500ml hot chicken stock
large pinch of saffron
100g fresh or frozen peas, defrosted if frozen
225g raw peeled jumbo prawns, defrosted if frozen
few stalks of thyme or rosemary
300g mussels (optional), cleaned and debearded
salt and pepper

Heat the oils in a large, wide sauté pan or paella pan (if you don't have any chilli oil just use a little more vegetable oil). Add the onions and cook, stirring, for about 5 minutes over a medium heat until golden.

Toss the chicken pieces in the paprika and add to the pan. Sizzle and stir for a few minutes until the chicken pieces are browned. Add the garlic, chorizo and peppers and stir-fry for 1-2 minutes.

Add the rice and stir to coat well. Add the wine, hot stock and saffron and give it all a good stir, then leave to simmer, uncovered, for about 15 minutes. Don't be tempted to stir it again – hard, I know but if it catches a little all the better. (In Spain a slightly crispy layer of rice on the bottom of the pan is known as the 'socarrat' and is completely authentic... so they tell me...) Scatter over the peas and push the prawns and thyme or rosemary stalks into the rice, as well as the mussels, if using (discard any mussels that do not close when tapped sharply). Season to taste.

Cover the pan with a lid or foil (to allow the mussels to steam) and cook for a further 7–8 minutes. Take a peek to make sure everything looks cooked – you may need to add a little more stock. Chuck out any mussels that haven't opened, then turn off the heat and leave to rest for a few minutes before serving.

Done. Can you believe it?

A recipe that has the words 'sweet', 'sticky' and 'nutty' in its name is surely going to attract anyone's attention. Unless you've got a nut allergy, in which case ignore this page and move swiftly on...

Sweet 'n' Sticky Nutty Chicken

Prepare in 20 mins · Cook in 50 mins · Serves 4–6

900g boneless and skinless chicken (breast and thigh), cut into bite-sized pieces
2 tbsp soya sauce
1 heaped tsp ground ginger
1 heaped tsp garlic paste
2 tsp soft brown sugar
125g unsalted peanuts
1 tbsp vegetable oil
1 tbsp sesame oil
8 spring onions, trimmed and cut into 4cm lengths
1 large red chilli, deseeded and finely chopped
2 tsp cornflour
2 tbsp mirin (Japanese cooking wine) or dry sherry
2 tbsp rice vinegar
200ml chicken stock
juice of ½ lime
juice of ½ lemon
½ tsp chilli flakes
100g bean sprouts

This is one to prepare in the morning if you can, so it has all day to marinate. Place the chicken pieces in a large non-metallic bowl and add the soya sauce, ground ginger, garlic and sugar. Mix really well, cover and marinate in the fridge for at least 1 hour, but 8 hours is ideal.

Preheat the oven to 180°C/160°C fan/Gas 4. Put the peanuts into a small roasting tin and roast in the oven for about 15 minutes, giving the tin a shake a couple of times. Allow to cool and then place in a plastic bag and bash with a rolling pin until they are lightly crushed. Set aside.

Heat a wok until really hot and then add your vegetable and sesame oils. Add the spring onion and chilli, then stir-fry for a minute. Toss your marinated chicken in the cornflour and then add to the wok with the remaining marinade. Stir-fry for about 7–8 minutes until browned all over.

Meanwhile, mix together the mirin, rice vinegar, chicken stock, lime juice, lemon juice and chilli flakes and add to the wok. Bring to the boil, then reduce the heat and simmer, uncovered, for about 25–30 minutes, stirring regularly. As the liquid reduces down the sauce will get good and sticky and start coating the chicken.

Stir through the bean sprouts, scatter the bashed peanuts over the top and serve.

Last time I made this I served it with some beautiful, mad purple carrots I'd found at a farmer's market. I split them lengthways and roasted them in olive oil and lemon juice. Took about 20–25 minutes in a hot oven. Walt said I should have done noodles...

There's something about barbecue chicken that is terrifically appealing at any time of the year. In the winter months this would go down a bomb with rice or potatoes of any sort, and in the summer months, sizzle the slathered chicken pieces on a barbecue and serve with blue cheese coleslaw (see page 142).

Saucy B.B.Q. Chicken

Prepare in 30 mins · Cook in 50 mins · Serves 6–8

2 x 1.8kg whole chickens
2 tbsp chilli oil
juice of 1 lemon (keep the squeezed halves)
salt and pepper

FOR THE BARBECUE SAUCE
4 tbsp tomato ketchup
1 tbsp tomato purée
2 tbsp light soya sauce
1 tbsp Dijon mustard
4 tsp sweet chilli sauce
1 tsp aged balsamic vinegar
few shakes of Tabasco
1 tbsp black treacle
1 tbsp demerara sugar
200ml Southern Comfort

Preheat the oven to 200°C/180°C fan/Gas 6.

First joint the chicken into breast, leg and thigh portions. You can ask your butcher to do this for you but if you do it yourself you will have a carcass to make lovely stock with. Remove all the skin from your chicken pieces and place the pieces in a large roasting tin. Drizzle over the chilli oil and lemon juice, keeping the squeezed halves,

season with salt and pepper and use your hands to mix everything together. Roast in the oven for 25 minutes.

While the chicken is in the oven make the barbecue sauce. Place all the sauce ingredients in a medium pan, along with the squeezed lemon halves. Stir over a medium heat until everything is combined and then let it bubble for 15–20 minutes, stirring occasionally, until you have a thick, sticky sauce.

When the chicken has been in for 25 minutes, remove from the oven and increase the temperature to 220°C/200°C fan/Gas 7. Pour off any juices that have collected in the roasting tin (add to your stock pot) and then slather the chicken pieces with the barbecue sauce, making sure they are all coated. Return to the oven for 20–25 minutes to get really nice and sticky, turning and basting after 10 minutes.

Be prepared for saucy cheeks... that's all I'm saying.

This recipe is one of those that came about because of what we had left in the fridge – there's often a bit of halloumi lurking that I have forgotten about. I feel it is a humble cheese, a bit like mozzarella, welcoming in the flavours around it like a self-effacing host. Hark at me and my cheese metaphors!

Halloumi, Salami & Pepper
Stuffed Chicken Breasts

Prepare in 20 mins · Cook in 25 mins · Serves 4

3 tbsp vegetable or olive oil
4 skinless and boneless chicken breast
    fillets
1 tbsp light soya sauce
1 red pepper, deseeded
100g halloumi, roughly chopped
6–8 slices of salami
4 large sage or basil leaves
750g potatoes, peeled and diced
herb salt (optional)
juice of 1 lemon
salt and pepper
½ quantity of Tomato Sauce (see page 95),
    to serve

Preheat the oven to 200°C/180°C fan/Gas 6.

Heat 1 tablespoon of oil in a large frying pan until hot and add the chicken breasts. Season lightly and brown on both sides over a high heat – this should take about 2 minutes. Add the soya sauce for the last 30 seconds. Transfer to a plate to cool slightly.

Place the red pepper and halloumi in a food processor and pulse to chop finely. Add the salami and pulse again briefly to combine. (You can do this by hand by just chopping very finely.)

Take your chicken breasts and slice them along the middle, but not all the way through, so you have a little chicken 'pitta'. Use the stuffing to fill each one, adding a sage or basil leaf to each pocket. Place in a small roasting tin, open side up. Bake in the oven for 20–25 minutes, until the chicken is cooked through and the cheese is melty.

Meanwhile, cook the potatoes. Heat the remaining oil in the pan, add the potatoes and season with salt and pepper – if you have any herb salt it will be delicious here. Toss to coat in the oil and then add the lemon juice. Cover the pan and cook over a low-medium heat for 15–20 minutes. Check them every so often to make sure they don't catch.

Gently heat the tomato sauce in a small pan. To serve, place a generous spoon of tomato sauce on each plate, top with a stuffed chicken breast and serve the potatoes on the side.

Note: If you fancy something green with this, steamed broccoli, tossed in a knob of butter and salt and pepper, does the trick.

This one was invented for comfort, and is great when the boys have a day-off-school sort of cold. When I first made it for them I went mad with the garlic and ginger but kept quiet about the cream (they have never been keen on cream) – sorry boys. It was a white lie that paid off though, because they liked it!

Garlic, Coconut & Chicken Korma

Prepare in 20 mins · Cook in 50 mins · Serves 4

**1.8–2kg whole chicken, jointed (ask your
butcher to do this for you*)**
2 tbsp vegetable oil
generous knob of butter
1 onion, thinly sliced
6 garlic cloves, crushed
1 heaped tsp ground ginger
1 heaped tsp ground cumin
1 heaped tsp ground turmeric
½ tsp ground cloves
1 tsp palm sugar
**1 tsp fenugreek seeds, crushed with a pestle
and mortar**
500ml chicken stock
1 tbsp desiccated coconut
1 tbsp ground almonds
zest and juice of 1 small lemon
2–3 tbsp double cream
salt and pepper

Season the chicken pieces all over with salt and pepper. Heat half the oil and the butter in a large deep sauté pan and add the chicken. Brown all over and then transfer to a plate – this should take about 10 minutes.

Add a little more oil to the pan, if needed, and then add the sliced onion. Cook gently for 10 minutes until golden. Add the garlic and stir for 1 minute.

Add the ginger, cumin, turmeric, cloves, sugar and fenugreek seeds and cook, stirring continuously, for 2 minutes. Then add the stock and bring to a simmer. Return the chicken pieces to the pan, submerging them in the liquid, and cover with a lid. Reduce the heat and simmer for 20 minutes, or until the chicken is cooked through.

For a deliciously velvety sauce, remove the chicken pieces and use a stick blender to whizz the sauce until smooth. Stir in the desiccated coconut, ground almonds, lemon zest and cream and simmer rapidly for about 5 minutes, until thickened. Return the chicken pieces, cook for a few more minutes to heat and then stir in the lemon juice.

Serve with your favourite curry accompaniments: plain boiled rice, steamed broccoli garnished with toasted almonds, naan bread/flatbreads... gorgeous.

* Before I did *MasterChef* the boys at our wonderful local butcher, Midhursts, welcomed me in as an apprentice to learn to do this. It's extremely satisfying, I find. Thank you so much Dave, Gary, Big Bob, Al and all – for that, and the meat on our table.

I am utterly mad about rice noodles, partly because I am one of those people with a bit of a pesky gluten intolerance. I couldn't believe it when I discovered them relatively late in life, in a Vietnamese eatery in Soho. But like a new word, once discovered I realised they were everywhere and that, actually, you can cook them at home! JOY. So I do. Often. This is the Lumsden (my married name!) version of a spicy noodle laksa.

Lumsden Laksa

Prepare in 15 mins · Cook in 15 mins · Serves 2–4

1 tbsp vegetable oil
1 tbsp sesame oil
1 stick of lemon grass, half finely chopped, other half bruised
3 spring onions, chopped
2 garlic cloves, finely chopped
thumb-sized piece of fresh ginger, peeled and finely chopped
1 red chilli, deseeded and finely chopped
2 chicken breasts, sliced
150g large raw peeled prawns
500ml chicken stock
400ml can coconut milk
juice of ½ lime (save the squeezed lime half)
1–2 tbsp fish sauce
1 tsp tomato purée
1 tsp peanut butter
1 tsp palm sugar or light brown sugar
½ tsp ground turmeric or a few strands of saffron (optional)
200g dried rice noodles
coriander leaves, to garnish

Heat both the oils in a large pan and add the chopped lemon grass, spring onions, garlic, ginger and red chilli. Stir-fry over a low-medium heat for 2 minutes.

Add the chicken and prawns and cook for a further 2–3 minutes, until coloured. Pour in the stock, coconut milk and lime juice and bring to a good simmer. Throw in the remaining lemon grass and the squeezed lime half.

Add a tablespoon of fish sauce, the tomato purée, peanut butter, sugar and turmeric or saffron, if using (the turmeric or saffron will give the soup a lovely deep colour but are not essential). Simmer the soup gently for about 10 minutes.

Meanwhile, place the rice noodles in a bowl and cover with boiling water; leave for 5 minutes, then drain and add to the soup. Mix well and taste, adding more fish sauce or a squeeze of lime if you think it needs it.

Serve ladled into deep bowls and garnish with coriander.

G

Spare Ribs – Ingredients

2½ lb. spare ribs of pork
3/4 pt. water
4 tbsps. soya sauce
(Salt to taste)

3 tbsps sugar n HONEY
3 tbsps. vinegar
1 tbsp. cornflour dissolved in
¼ pt. water
2 tbsps dry sherry
1 level teasp. fresh grated ginger root.

(on top)
Cook ribs in water w. soya sauce +
salt. Bring to boil then simmer for 1hr
Transfer to shallow pan, or frying pan
Add remaining ingredients +
fry till gravy translucent

LANGHAM PLACE, REGENT STREET, LONDON W1N 8QS
TELEPHONE: 020 7580 0111 FACSIMILE: 020 7436 7997

Lambs, Beefs, Pigs & A game

I'm a sucker for slow cooking. (That's the thing that threw me most on *MasterChef*: the speed at which you have to do things.) The smells that emanate; the fact that you can prepare well in advance and it just gets better and better; the do-it-in-the-morning approach... and then, just when you're thinking about having to rustle up some nosh and you're feeling weary and uninspired, you remember that it's all sorted – what joy. All you have to do is boil up a few tatties or a bit of rice.

Mum's Saucy Shanx

Prepare in 40 mins · Cook in 4 hours · Serves 4

1.2kg tomatoes (about 12)
2 tbsp light brown sugar
1 tbsp tomato purée
1 tbsp dried oregano or mixed herbs
50g can of anchovy fillets
1 onion, finely chopped
1 red chilli, deseeded and chopped
2 tbsp aged syrupy balsamic vinegar
1 tbsp vegetable oil
4 lamb shanks, about 300–350g each
2 tbsp dark soya sauce
about 300ml white wine
3 bay leaves
salt and pepper

Preheat the oven to 130°C/120°C fan/Gas 1.

Score a cross through the skin of each tomato, place in a large bowl and cover with boiling water. Leave for a few minutes then place in a bowl of cold water. Slip the skins off and then chop the tomatoes finely and place in a large pan. (If you can't be doing with these tomato shenanigans you can skip this part and use canned chopped tomatoes instead.) Add the sugar, tomato purée, herbs and seasoning and bring to the boil. Reduce the heat and simmer, uncovered, for about 20 minutes, stirring occasionally.

Place a frying pan over a medium heat and add the oil from the canned anchovies. Add the onion and fry for 7–8 minutes, to soften. Finely chop the anchovies and add to the onions with the chilli. Cook for a further 5 minutes, then stir in the balsamic vinegar and set aside.

Heat the vegetable oil in a large flameproof casserole. Season the lamb shanks all over and then brown over a medium-high heat, turning to brown on all sides. This should take about 10 minutes. Add the soya sauce for the final minute.

Add the onion mix to the thickened tomatoes and stir together, then add the white wine and bay leaves. Pour it over the shanks, cover and transfer to the oven. Cook for at least 3 or 4 hours. The longer and slower the better, so if you want to cook for 5 hours just reduce the oven temperature a bit more.

These shanks are just gorgeous with creamy mustard mash.

This dish is rich and fragrant and the flavours meld together beautifully. It's fun to assemble and oh, how we love lamb and oh, how we love those warming spices and the aromas that ensue. This is a slow-cooked wonder that does just what it says on the... oh goodie, it's not from a tin.

Spicey Ricey
Lamb Shoulder

Prepare in 20 mins · Cook in 2½ hours, plus resting · Serves 6–8

1.5kg boned lamb shoulder (ask your butcher to bone a shoulder for you)
200g long-grain or basmati rice
2 tsp bouillon powder
30g golden raisins, chopped (any raisins will do; I just love these)
1 tsp ground ginger
1 tsp ground cinnamon
1 tsp ground coriander
2 large garlic cloves, crushed
20g soft butter
4 rosemary sprigs
150ml dry white wine
salt and pepper

Remove your lamb from the fridge at least an hour before cooking.

Cook the rice in a large pan of boiling water to which you have added 1 teaspoon of bouillon powder. Drain well and allow to cool. Preheat the oven to 200°C/180°C fan/ Gas 6.

Place the cooked rice in a bowl and mix in the raisins, remaining bouillon, ground spices and garlic.

Open up your shoulder and season lightly. Tip the spicy rice on to the lamb, stuffing it into all the crevices. Roll the joint up and tie with string a few times down the length of the joint.

Place in a large roasting tin, dot with butter, lightly season and tuck the rosemary sprigs under the string. Cover the tin tightly with foil and cook in the oven for 2 hours, basting a couple of times.

Remove the foil after 2 hours and pour the wine into the roasting tin. Stir into the juices and then return the tin to the oven for another 30 minutes.

Take out of the oven and leave to rest for 15 minutes, covered in foil, before carving into thick slices. Serve with some cooked peas that you have roughly squished with a knob of butter, a few chopped mint leaves and some salt and pepper. Gladsomeness abounding.

Again we are on a 'go slow'. That's how it should be on a Sunday, let's face it. If you manage to get hold of a good bit of meat, this recipe really does do all the magic for you. All it needs is a few firm friends to party with in the heat of your oven.

Slow Roast Sunday Lamb

Prepare in 15 mins · Cook in 4¼ hours, plus resting · Serves 8

2kg whole leg of lamb
2 tbsp olive oil
6 shallots, peeled
6 garlic cloves
4 rashers smoked streaky bacon, chopped
2–3 bay leaves
2–3 rosemary sprigs
30g golden raisins
8 dried apricots
1 bottle dry white wine
1 tbsp aged balsamic vinegar
350ml water
1 tbsp cornflour
salt and pepper

Preheat the oven to 170°C/150°C fan/Gas 3½. Decide what you are going to cook the lamb in – I like to use a large flameproof casserole dish so the lamb is nestling in the lovely juices, but you could do this in a deep-sided roasting tray.

Season the lamb all over with salt and pepper. Place a large, flameproof roasting tray over a medium heat and add the oil. Brown the leg of lamb, turning regularly with tongs to brown all over – this will take about 8–10 minutes. Remove from the pan and set aside.

Add the whole shallots, garlic cloves and bacon to the roasting tray and brown for 2–3 minutes, stirring continuously. If you are cooking in the roasting tray, return the lamb to the tray, add the bay leaves, rosemary sprigs, golden raisins, apricots, white wine, balsamic vinegar and water and bring to a simmer. Cover loosely with foil and place in the oven. Alternatively, transfer everything to a large casserole dish, cover with the lid and place in the oven.

After 4 hours the lamb will be lovely and tender but if you have more time and can bear to wait, you could easily give this another hour – it will just be even more meltingly tender.

When cooked, remove from the oven and set the lamb aside while you make the gravy. Skim any fat off the top of the cooking juices, using a large spoon. Mix a little of the liquid with the cornflour to make a smooth paste and then add this back to the sauce. Cook over a low heat for a few minutes to thicken, then taste and adjust the seasoning. You can either serve the gravy as it is or strain it to remove the now not so dried fruits!

Serve the lamb with heaps of roast tatties to mop up the gravy, roasted vegetables and buttery spinach. For some reason this dish always raises a smile. There's something a tad audacious about a whole leg of lamb with so much gravy.

This is yet another one of those slow-cooked dishes that I love (and why not – there's enough 'fast food' about – let's redress the balance and take our time), as once you have put it all together you can forget about it, while the fragrance dabs its perfume around the lobes of your house...! The muse for this dish is our amazing local curry house, Majjo's.

Lamb & Beetroot Curry

Prepare in 20 mins · Cook in 3 hours · Serves 4

1kg boneless lamb from the leg, cut
   into 5cm pieces
1 tbsp vegetable oil
1 heaped tbsp panch phoran
8 cardamom pods, lightly crushed
   with a pestle and mortar
1 tsp ground coriander
2 tsp mild chilli powder
1 tsp palm sugar
1 tsp tamarind paste
400g (about 4 medium) raw beetroot, peeled
   and grated
400ml water
salt and pepper

Preheat the oven to 140°C/120°C fan/Gas 1.

Brown the lamb in two batches in a large frying pan over a medium-high heat, using half the oil for each batch. Make sure the pieces are browned on all sides. Transfer to a large flameproof casserole dish.

Lightly crush the panch phoran and cardamom pods with a pestle and mortar.

(Panch phoran is a Bengali spice mix made up of cumin, fenugreek, mustard, fennel and black onion seeds. I bought it once because I loved the name, but if you don't have it in your cupboard, just use any spices from this list that you do have.)

Add the spices to the lamb along with the ground coriander and chilli powder, then place the casserole over a medium-high heat and cook, stirring, for 2 minutes.

Add the palm sugar, tamarind paste, grated beetroot and water and bring to the boil. Cover with a lid and transfer to the oven. Cook for 2½ –3 hours, checking occasionally and adding a little more water if needed – beetroots vary in their juiciness... don't we all? Taste and adjust the seasoning before serving.

I serve this with some mango chutney, raita and naan bread.

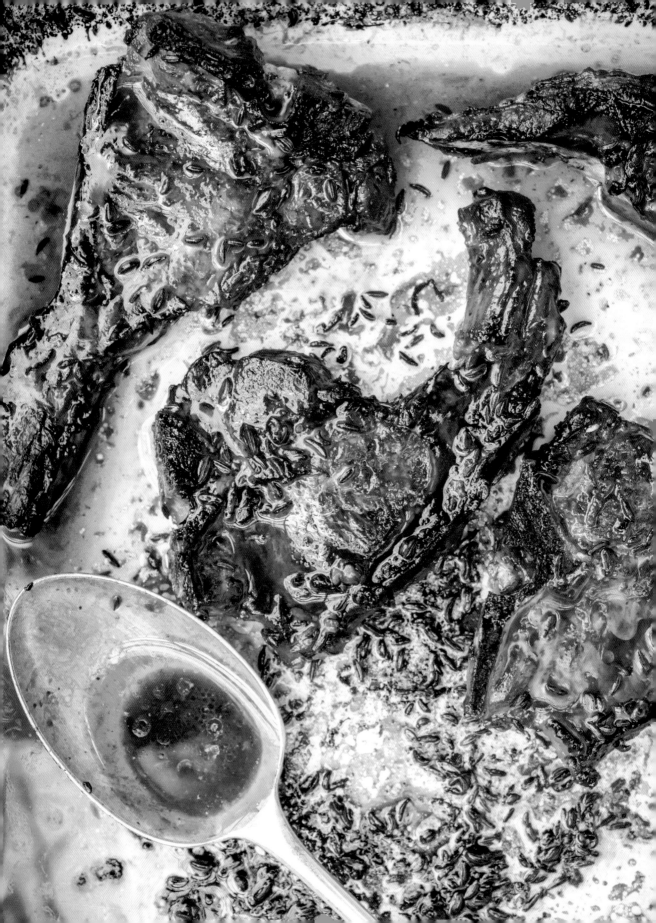

Any food I can eat with my hands gets the thumbs up as far as I'm concerned. The chop is a classic. You simply HAVE to pick them up and have a good old gnaw. Not necessarily a first date choice, but definitely a third date.

Cumin Caraway Chops

Prepare in 10 mins, plus 30 mins marinating · Cook in 20 mins · Serves 2

FOR THE LAMB
30g butter
1 tsp honey
1 tsp cumin seeds, crushed with a
   pestle and mortar
1 tsp caraway seeds, crushed with a
   pestle and mortar
4 x 150g lamb chops
salt and pepper

FOR THE RICE
1 tsp vegetable bouillon powder
100g basmati or long-grain rice
1 tbsp vegetable oil
1 tsp butter
1 onion, finely chopped
1 tsp ground turmeric
½ tsp mixed spice
zest of 1 lemon
2 handfuls of peas, defrosted if frozen

Put the butter, honey, cumin and caraway seeds into a small pan with some salt and pepper and heat gently until combined. Place the chops in a shallow dish and pour over the marinade, turning to coat all over. Leave to marinate at room temperature (you don't want the butter to harden) for at least 30 minutes but up to an hour if possible. Turn every now and then – if you remember – so the lamb becomes lovely and moist.

Make the spicey rice by bringing a pan of water to the boil. Stir in the bouillon powder and then add the rice. Cook for about 8–10 minutes until just tender. Drain, rinse in boiling water and leave to steam in a colander.

Preheat the grill to its highest setting. Put the marinated chops in a small roasting tin and place under the grill. Cook for 3 minutes each side for medium and 4 minutes each side for well done. I like my chops nicely charred – almost burnt!

Meanwhile, heat the oil and butter in a large pan and fry the onion over a medium heat for about 6 minutes, until softened. Stir in the turmeric, mixed spice, lemon zest and peas and cook for a couple of minutes. Add your cooked and drained rice and stir until well combined.

Serve your juicy cumin and caraway chops with your spicey rice, spooning over the buttery sauce from the roasting tin.

It's gnawing time.

For years I was a bit obsessed with *Coronation Street* and the wonderful women in it... Barbara Knox, Jean Alexander, Betty Driver, to name but three. I always rather fantasised about Betty's Hotpot in the Rover's Return. This is my homage to Betty. I hope she would raise a milk stout to it.

Betty's Hot Pot

Prepare in 15 mins · Cook in 2 hours 50 mins · Serves 4

1 tbsp vegetable oil
500g lamb neck fillet, trimmed and cut into 3–4cm pieces
40g butter, plus extra for the top
3 onions, thinly sliced
2 leeks, trimmed, rinsed and roughly chopped
2 carrots, roughly chopped
2 celery sticks, roughly chopped on the diagonal
2 bay leaves
1 tbsp finely chopped thyme leaves, plus a few sprigs
500g potatoes (about 4), peeled and sliced into 8mm thick slices
rosemary sprig (optional), leaves picked
500ml hot chicken stock
salt and pepper

Preheat the oven to 180°C/160°C fan/Gas 4.

Heat the oil in a large flameproof casserole dish. Season the lamb pieces and brown them all over for about 5 minutes, turning often. Remove and set aside.

Add about half the butter to the oil already in the casserole and add the sliced onions. Cook over a medium heat for about 10 minutes, until soft and glistening. Season with salt and pepper, then remove with a slotted spoon and set aside.

Add the remaining butter to the casserole and sweat the leeks, carrots and celery for about 5 minutes. Add the bay leaves, chopped thyme and a little more seasoning.

Leave the vegetables and herbs in the base of the casserole and layer your glistening onions over the top, followed by a layer of all the browned meat. Arrange the sliced potatoes on top of the meat, dotting with butter here and there and adding a few more thyme leaves and some rosemary leaves if you fancy. (I like a mix of herbs, but stick with one if you prefer.)

Season well with salt and pepper and then pour over the hot stock. Put the lid on and cook in the oven for 2 hours, basting the top of the potatoes with some of the juices a couple of times, so they turn lovely and shiny. If you want a slightly crisper potato topping, remove the lid for the last 20 minutes or so.

Note: I tried this adding a lamb cutlet or four to the lamb fillet – inspired by a version I had in a gastropub once – dem bones definitely gave it a bit of extra 'Corrie' drama!

We made these one autumn when we were madly trying to use as many of the apples from our tree as we could. The recipe only uses one, but every little helps! An apple is a lovely addition to a burger, like a secret inbuilt autumn relish. It also slightly lightens the mix, not to mention the juiciness it imbues...

Walter is the official burger cook in our house, and will add bacon, cheese or tomato to order.

Autumn Burgers

Prepare in 15 mins, plus chilling · Cook in 15 mins · Serves 4

2 smallish carrots, peeled
1 small eating apple, peeled and cored
400g beef mince
1 tsp syrupy aged balsamic vinegar
½ tsp celery salt
1 tsp dried oregano or dried mixed herbs
2 heaped tsp tomato purée
½ tsp cayenne pepper (if you can find sweet cayenne pepper, use it here)
20g fresh breadcrumbs
black pepper

Grate the carrots and apple and then use your hands to squeeze out any excess juice. Put the squeezed carrot and apple into a large bowl. Add all the remaining ingredients and mix together with your hands until well combined. The apple and carrot should make the mixture feel quite moist but the breadcrumbs will help hold it together.

Divide and shape the mixture into four burgers. Place on a plate, cover with cling film and chill for at least 30 minutes (you could make these up to a day in advance).

When you are ready to cook, place a large non-stick frying pan over a medium-high heat. Add the burgers and cook for about 10–15 minutes, depending on how well done you like your meat. Turn regularly so they cook nice and evenly.

The boys love these in a bun with some melted Cheddar and a few potato wedges on the side.

This is definitely one to prep the day before, as there are two stages to this unusual and delicious concoction, but don't let that put you off. It's fantastically homely. I'd never heard of this curious South African dish until I stayed with the wonderful Sally Rieder when I was working in Chichester on a production of *Guys and Dolls*. Sally was on the 'digs list' – you can never be sure what you are going to get. Lucky for me, I picked a corker. Sally called me 'Mole' because I stayed in her basement. I called her 'Landlady' – I don't know how I came up with that one.

Sally's Babotie

Prepare in 30 mins, plus chilling · Cook in 1½ hours · Serves 6–8

50g butter
2 onions, finely chopped
2 tbsp mild curry powder
2 tsp ground turmeric
1 large garlic clove, crushed
1 heaped tsp chopped fresh ginger
1 heaped tsp ground ginger
1 green chilli (the hot ones), deseeded
   and finely chopped
30g brown sugar
2 slices of white bread, crusts removed
125ml milk
1kg minced beef
juice of ½ lemon
25g golden raisins or sultanas
10 dried apricots, chopped
generous grating of nutmeg
¼ tsp allspice
30g toasted flaked almonds
3 bay leaves
3 eggs
2 tbsp milk
salt and pepper

Melt the butter in a large, wide frying pan and add the onions. Cook gently over a low heat for 12–15 minutes, to soften. Stir in the curry powder, turmeric, garlic, fresh and ground ginger, chilli and brown sugar and continue to cook for a few minutes more. Set aside. Meanwhile, place the bread in a bowl, cover with the milk and leave to soak for

5–10 minutes. Add the soaked bread to the onions and spices. Gradually add the minced beef, a handful at a time, stirring to brown the meat as it's added. Add the lemon juice, golden raisins, chopped apricots, nutmeg, allspice and flaked almonds. Add 175ml water to the pan to loosen the mixture and cook gently for 10–15 minutes. Taste and adjust the seasoning.

Transfer to a medium ovenproof baking dish and smooth the surface, pressing the bay leaves into the top. Cool, cover and chill in the fridge overnight.

The next day you will open the fridge and think, 'Oh joy, I have the makings of a babotie here!' Preheat the oven to 200°C/180°C fan/Gas 6. Lightly whisk together the eggs and milk and some salt and pepper. Pour over the chilled mince mixture and bake in the oven for 45 minutes, or until golden and cooked through. I like to serve this with rice, but Sally says it's also terrific with a tomato and onion sambul (a simple salad of chopped red onions and tomatoes). Simply chop a small red onion and some interesting tomatoes and dress with olive oil, red wine vinegar and fresh basil leaves. Thank you Sal and South Africa!

This is a great alternative to a Sunday roast; a one-pan wonder that you can plonk on the table. I make all the elements the day before; on the day you just introduce them to each other, and they remember how well they all get on. A big green salad with some chicory, avocado and sunflower seeds is a boon, adding crunch to your soft, saucy main.

Big Sunday Lasagne

Prepare in 50 mins · Cook in 1¾ hours · Serves 8

FOR THE TOMATO SAUCE
2 tbsp olive oil
4 x 400g cans chopped tomatoes
1 tbsp dried oregano
1 tbsp light muscovado sugar
salt and pepper

FOR THE MEAT
1.5kg beef mince
2–3 tbsp olive oil
2 tsp light muscovado sugar
2 tsp Dijon mustard
1 tbsp sun-dried tomato paste
1 tbsp tomato purée
2 tbsp tomato ketchup
1 tsp garlic paste (from a tube)
1 tbsp Worcestershire sauce
1 tbsp soya sauce

FOR THE WHITE SAUCE
50g butter
50g plain flour
800ml milk
2 tsp Dijon mustard
2 tsp Worcestershire sauce
2 tsp soya sauce
generous grating of nutmeg
200g mature Cheddar, grated

TO ASSEMBLE
about 200g dried lasagne sheets
small handful of fresh basil leaves
2–3 tomatoes, thinly sliced
50g mature Cheddar, grated

First make the tomato sauce. Heat the olive oil in a large pan and add the chopped tomatoes, oregano, sugar and a generous amount of salt and pepper. Bring to a gentle simmer and then cook, uncovered, for about 30 minutes.

Meanwhile, brown the beef in a large frying pan over a high heat. You will need to do this in batches, so use a little oil each time and wipe out the pan between batches. Return all the meat to the pan and add the remaining meat ingredients. Cook over a medium heat, stirring together, for about 2 minutes. Transfer to a bowl and allow to cool – if you are making this the day before, cover and keep in the fridge until you are ready to assemble.

Next make the white sauce. Melt the butter in a pan and stir in the flour. Let this roux cook for a couple of minutes and then start adding the milk in stages, whisking into the roux. Continue adding and whisking over a low heat until you have smooth sauce. Remove from the heat and add all the remaining ingredients. Stir until well combined and then taste and adjust the seasoning. Set aside until ready to use.

When you are ready to assemble, preheat the oven to 180°C/160°C fan/Gas 4 and find a suitable large ovenproof dish.

Spoon and spread about one-third of the meat over the base of the dish. Follow this with a quarter of the tomato sauce, a quarter of the white sauce and a few torn basil leaves. Then top with your lasagne sheets. Repeat these layers, finishing with an extra layer of tomato and white sauce. Top with the sliced tomatoes and grated Cheddar.

Cover with foil and cook on the middle shelf of the oven for about 45 minutes. Remove the foil and return to the oven for a further 15–20 minutes to brown up nicely. If it's not bubbling and golden enough for your liking, give it a few minutes under a really hot grill.

Roll up, roll up, hungry peeps!

Mince in all its forms has got to win some sort of prize for adaptability. Meatballs and tomato sauce are as fabulous together as toad and hole, ice cream and cornet, and Eric and Ernie, to name but three.

The Boys' Meatballs

Prepare in 45 mins, plus chilling · Cook in 1 hour 10 mins · Makes 18–20

FOR THE MEATBALLS
1kg beef mince
2 tsp garlic paste (from a handy tube)
2 tsp sun-dried tomato paste
2 tsp dried oregano
2 tsp dried basil
2 generous tsp grainy mustard
1 tsp ground mace
1 tsp sweet smoked paprika
2 tsp redcurrant jelly
200g fresh breadcrumbs
2 tbsp plain flour
2 tsp celery salt
2–3 tbsp olive oil, for frying
3–4 tsp light soya sauce, to season

FOR THE TOMATO SAUCE
1 tbsp olive oil
1 large onion, chopped
2 garlic cloves, chopped
100ml fruity red wine
2 x 400g cans chopped tomatoes
400ml V8 vegetable juice
2 bay leaves
2 tsp brown sugar
salt and pepper

Make the meatballs by mixing the beef, garlic paste, sun-dried tomato paste, oregano, basil, mustard, ground mace, smoked paprika and redcurrant jelly together in a large bowl. Get in there with your hands to make sure the mixture is well combined. Mix the breadcrumbs, flour and celery salt together on your work surface. Shape the meat mixture into balls – you should get about 18–20 balls, depending on

how big you make them. Roll each ball in the breadcrumb mixture and place on a tray. Chill in the fridge for 30 minutes.

Meanwhile, make the tomato sauce. Heat the oil in a large pan, add the onion and cook over a low heat for 10 minutes, or until softened. Add the garlic and cook for a few moments before adding the wine; let it bubble for a minute. Add the chopped tomatoes, vegetable juice, bay leaves, sugar and salt and pepper. Stir well and leave to simmer for 30 minutes to reduce down a bit.

When it looks sufficiently saucy, remove the bay leaves and blitz with a hand blender so you are left with a lovely, thick, tomato sauce crying out for a meatball. I put the bay leaves back in at this point and leave the sauce sitting over a very gentle heat.

To cook the meatballs, heat the oil in a large frying pan over a medium-high heat and fry in batches until browned all over – this takes about 6–8 minutes per batch. Turn the meatballs carefully, using tongs or a couple of wooden spoons. Add a splash of soya sauce towards the end of cooking each batch, to add colour and seasoning. Remove from the pan with a slotted spoon, drain on kitchen paper briefly and then snuggle them into your pan of sauce. Cover and cook very gently for 15-20 minutes.

These are so versatile you could serve them with rice and salad, mash, pasta or indeed chips from the chippy.

Mum's mince was the traditional fare we had when we came home from school holidays, or from anywhere we'd been for more than a week! It was served in a big pot on the table, always with slow-baked potatoes. It was my absolute favourite meal. Now it is one of my boys' faves, although they prefer it with rice.

Because Mum is Scottish, we always use Scottish mince, which our brilliant butcher always stocks, but obviously there are other minces available of very fine repute.

Moomin's Mince

Prepare in 10 mins · Cook in 50 mins · Serves 8

1 tbsp olive oil
1 tbsp vegetable oil
1kg beef mince
2 tsp Dijon mustard
2 tsp Worcestershire sauce
2 tsp dark soya sauce
2 tsp dark muscovado sugar
150ml red wine
300ml V8 vegetable juice
salt and pepper

Heat the oils in a large, heavy-based pan over a low-medium heat. Add the mince and brown thoroughly (in batches if your pan looks a bit crowded).

When all the meat is browned, add the mustard, Worcestershire sauce, soya sauce and sugar. Stir to combine and then pour in the wine and let it simmer for a minute. Add the V8 and some salt and pepper and bring back to a simmer. Cover and cook gently for 30–40 minutes. Taste and adjust the seasoning, adding salt and pepper or more soya or Worcestershire sauce as you see fit.

As I have said, we love Moomin's mince as it is, with baked potatoes or rice. But it also makes a fantastic base for cottage pie – individual or family sized. Just top with buttery mash and bake in the oven for about 30 minutes. Grated cheese topping a bonus, should you concur.

This is a quick-to-prep-then-slow-to-cook tea that our boys love. When Richard and I are both lucky enough to be in gainful employ at the same time, and both out all day, the slow cooker gets a good dusting down. It's a great one if you are going to be back late from work, as you can prepare it in the morning and leave it to do its thing, and then tea just miraculously appears. But not to worry if you don't have a slow cooker, as this is just as easy on the stovetop, which is where I usually make it due to the vagaries of our profession!

Mama's Jerk Beef

Prepare in 5 mins · Cook in 2 hours 20 mins · Serves 4

1kg braising beef, cut into 3cm cubes
2 generous tbsp jerk seasoning (there
** are some great varieties out there –**
** I use a powdered one)**
2 tbsp vegetable oil
400g can plum tomatoes
juice of 1 large orange
200g frozen peas
salt and pepper

Place the beef cubes in a large bowl and sprinkle over the jerk seasoning. Toss gently to coat well.

Heat the oil in a large frying pan and add the beef in batches over a medium heat, turning to brown on all sides. Transfer each batch to a large casserole dish.

Add the plum tomatoes and then fill the empty can with water and add that too (this ensures that not a drop of tomato juice is wasted). Bring up to a simmer, breaking up the tomatoes a bit with the back of a wooden spoon. Add the orange juice and seasoning and then cover and simmer over a low heat for 2 hours.

Add the frozen peas for the last 20 minutes of cooking time. Serve with plain rice, mash or baked potatoes.

This is a great thing to prep and have cold at a weekend lunch when the in-laws are rocking up, or there's a bit of a do and you want something easy to serve. It's a loaf of coarse pâté really, so break open those pickled onions (see page 46) and gherkins that are skulking in the cupboard, not to mention the chutney and the mustard. A good strong piece of Cheddar wouldn't go amiss either.

My Meaty Loaf

Prepare in 50 mins · Cook in 1½ hours · Serves 8

1 tbsp vegetable oil
1 large onion, finely chopped
1 large carrot, finely chopped
1 celery stick, finely chopped
3 garlic cloves, finely chopped
1 tbsp finely chopped thyme leaves
4 eggs
1 tbsp Dijon mustard
2 tbsp tomato ketchup
2 tbsp Worcestershire sauce
splash of Tabasco
½ tsp grated nutmeg
½ tsp cayenne pepper
¼ tsp ground allspice
4 sun-dried tomatoes in oil
500g beef mince
500g pork mince
125g fresh breadcrumbs
10–12 rashers smoked streaky bacon
4–6 Savoy cabbage leaves
salt and pepper

Preheat the oven to 200°C/180°C fan/Gas 6.

Heat the oil in a large frying pan and add the onion, carrot, celery and garlic. Cook gently for about 10 minutes until softened. Add the thyme and continue to cook for a few more minutes. Tip into a shallow bowl and set aside to cool.

In a large mixing bowl mix together the eggs, Dijon mustard, tomato ketchup, Worcestershire sauce, Tabasco and spices. Finely chop the sun-dried tomatoes (you'll need some oil from the jar later) and add to the bowl. Season with salt and pepper. Add the beef and pork mince and breadcrumbs and then the cooled vegetables. Use your hands to squidge it all together. →

Lightly oil a 1kg loaf tin with some of the sun-dried tomato oil and then use the bacon to line the base and sides of the tin. Fill the loaf tin almost to the top with your magic meaty mixture, pressing down well, and flip any overhanging bacon back over the top. Cover the top of the tin with a piece of baking paper and secure with string. Place the loaf tin in a deep roasting tray and half-fill the tray with boiling water. Carefully transfer to the oven and cook for 1¼ hours.

Remove the loaf tin from the tray and set the tray of hot water aside for now. Carefully remove the baking paper and drain away any liquid that is in the loaf tin. Preheat the grill to high. Turn your loaf out on to a lightly oiled baking tray and place under the grill for 8–10 minutes, or until the bacon is nicely browned.

Meanwhile take your Savoy cabbage leaves and cut away the tough central stalk. Place the leaves in the tray of hot water and leave to soften for a few minutes. Drain on kitchen paper and then arrange on a lovely serving dish. Place the meatloaf on top of the leaves.

Delicious hot or cold.

pickled onions

This is dedicated to Big Wal and Claire. Big Wal is really called Valentine, but for some reason everyone calls him Wal. He has been 'Big' Wal since our smaller Wal came into the world. Valentine Gould is a master restorer, an old pal of Mum and Dad's, and he used to have an antique shop in Bath. I'd visit when I was a drama student, and he and his Mrs, Claire, would take me out for some slap-up grub. Big Wal was born in Paddington Green, and sings old musical hall songs* to me. He had a canary called Kenny Domingo who sat on his shoulder and picked his teeth.

Strictly speaking I don't think beef olives normally include olives but when I hear the word 'olive', I'm keen to have an olive, so I've added them. Such a comforting dish. My Grandpa Jacko, who used to import eggs (packaging nightmare, I've always imagined) and who was, very luckily for him, married to Granny Megsie, loved them. How I wish Megsie was still around to tip me a particular wink and tell me exactly what she did. Well, you'll have to make do with my version.

Prepare in 20 mins · Cook in 2½–2¾ hours · Makes 4

FOR THE STUFFING
6 pork sausages
generous grating of nutmeg
1 tsp smoked paprika
1 tsp dried mixed herbs
1 tsp celery salt
12 black olives, stoned and chopped
black pepper

2 rump steaks, about 250g each,
**   trimmed of visible fat**
1–2 tbsp plain flour
2 tbsp olive oil
1 onion, chopped
1 tbsp tomato purée
1 tsp soft light brown sugar
400ml red wine
1 tbsp chopped fresh parsley,
**   to garnish**

First make the stuffing. Squeeze the sausagemeat out of the skins into a bowl. Add the nutmeg, smoked paprika, mixed herbs, celery salt and black olives. Add a little pepper to season and mix well to combine.

Bat out the rump steak, giving it a bit of a beating with a meat mallet or rolling pin (I sometimes ask my butcher to do this for me). This will tenderise the meat, as well as flatten it. Cut each piece into two so you have four thin pieces of beef.

Lightly dust your work surface with a bit of flour and lay your beef strips on top. Divide the stuffing mix between them and then roll up your lovely floury meat parcels. Secure each one with string – you will need about 2–3 pieces per beef olive. ➔

Heat the olive oil in a large frying pan and brown the beef olives for about 5 minutes, until golden on all sides. Transfer to a lidded casserole dish.

Add the chopped onion to the lovely, meaty frying pan (you may need a splash more oil) and cook for 5 minutes, until golden. Add the tomato purée and brown sugar and cook for 1 minute. Pour in the wine and bubble for 2 minutes. Add 250ml water and return to a simmer. Pour this over your beef olives in the casserole, cover and simmer very gently for 2–2½ hours (remove the lid for the last hour to reduce the gravy). Check on your olives occasionally but don't stir your sleeping beauties too much if you can help it.

Remove the string before scattering with parsley and serving – buttery mash with this gets my vote.

Boiled beef and carrots
Boiled beef and carrots
That's the stuff for your Derby Kell [1]
Makes you fit and keeps you well.

Don't live like vegetarians
On food they give to parrots
Blow out yer kite [2] *from morn 'til night*
On boiled beef and carrots. [3]

Thank you, Mr Valentine Gould Esquire.

[1] Derby Kelly is rhyming slang for belly.
[2] Fill your stomach.
[3] Or beef olives, obvs…

Mum tells me she got this recipe from a landlady in Coventry when she was on tour there years ago in a musical called *Murder in the Red Barn*. The mind boggles. When I was growing up and Mum said it was goulash for tea I was always very happy. (As opposed to when she said kedgeree, and I felt curiously mournful, although I love it now.) I love the colour and smell of goulash and the fact that we always had it with a big pile of white rice, which for some reason became my task to cook. I mysteriously garnered a reputation for being good with rice – I wasn't going to argue.

My boys Walter and Ernie love goulash too but they don't like the name; to them it sounds creamy and they have a deep dislike of creamy savouries. So we renamed it 'shaluog'... see what we almost did there?

Mum's Goulash

Prepare in 20 mins · Cook in 3½ hours · Serves 6

50g lard
2 tbsp goose fat
5 onions, thinly sliced (if you have a food processor with a slicer attachment, this is a great time to use it to avoid those tears)
3 tbsp sweet paprika
900g braising steak, cut into 3cm dice
1 tbsp olive oil
400g can chopped tomatoes
150ml Guinness
200ml V8 vegetable juice (or vegetable stock)
200ml water
sour cream or Greek yogurt, to serve
chopped chives (optional), to garnish
salt and pepper

Preheat the oven to 140°C/120°C fan/Gas 1.

Melt the lard and goose fat in a large casserole. Add the onions, cover and cook over a low heat for about 15 minutes, stirring occasionally, until soft. Add the

paprika (I know it seems loads) and cook for 5 minutes, stirring it in until you have wonderful orangey onions.

Meanwhile in a separate frying pan brown the beef in batches, using a small amount of olive oil for each batch. Transfer the browned beef to the casserole.

Add the chopped tomatoes, Guinness, vegetable juice (or stock) and water. Bring to the boil, give it a good stir, then cover and place in the oven for 1½ hours. After this time remove the lid, season to taste, and return to the oven for a further 1½ hours. The beef will be gloriously tender.

I like to serve this with lemony rice (which is simply cooked basmati stirred through with olive oil, lemon juice and salt and pepper) and a dollop of sour cream or Greek yogurt. A sprinkling of chives wouldn't go amiss.

Tenderloin is so wonderful – it's the fillet steak of the pork world. I think of this recipe as rather like 'dressing up' your tenderloin. It's simple but it looks, I reckon, rather special. I made this as my first 'Hello, this is me' food on *MasterChef* and I was shaking like a very shaky actress. The judges liked it, but I seem to remember I hadn't washed the carrots, and John Torode choked on a twig of thyme.

Pork Tenderloin in Pancetta

Prepare in 10 mins · Cook in 30 mins · Serves 4–6

150–175g thinly sliced pancetta (about 16–18 slices)
2 x 450g pork tenderloins, trimmed
2 tbsp olive oil
salt and pepper

FOR THE GRAVY
10g flour
knob of butter
1 tsp grainy mustard
150ml cider
½ tsp soya sauce
1 tbsp cream
a few thyme leaves

Preheat the oven to 200°C/180°C fan/Gas 6.

The pancetta here needs to be really thin, so ask for it to be cut super thin at your deli or deli counter. If you are buying in packets you may find it is thin enough already. If not, gently stretch each piece out with the back of a knife. Lay out half the pancetta slices on a wooden board, overlapping each other slightly, to make a sort of pancetta wallpaper. Or pork paper!

Season both pork loins and place one of them in the middle of the pancetta rectangle. Wrap the loin in the pancetta, pressing it so that it sticks and covers the loin. Repeat with the remaining loin and pork paper.

Heat the oil in a large frying pan and fry the pork loins until they are nicely browned all over – don't worry too much if the pancetta peels away a little, you can always press it back. Transfer to a roasting tin and cover with foil. Cook in the oven for about 20 minutes, depending on the thickness of the loin.

Remove from the oven and leave to rest for a good 10 minutes before carving into nice thick slices on the diagonal. Fabulous with mustard mash or Herby Boulangère Potatoes (see page 134) or some baby carrots roasted with thyme – just remove the thyme sprigs if you're adhering to health and safety.

You can make a really quick mustard and cider saucy gravy to go with this if you like. Just put a dessertspoon (approx 10g) of flour in a pan with a generous knob of butter, and/or some of the meat juices if there is plenty. Make a roux and heat stirring for a moment or two to cook off the flour. Add a tsp grainy mustard, and stir in 150ml dry cider (off the heat for a moment to avoid lumps), and the rest of the meat juices. Add half a tsp soya sauce, and a tablespoon of cream... a few thyme leaves never go amiss – not to mention some fresh ground pepper.

This is a lip-smacking, simple pork and rice dish that makes a brilliant all-in-one meal. If you've got any vegetarians at the table you can use tofu or another meat substitute, such as Quorn, instead of the pork. I just love a speedy tasty tea option, and when it involves a pineapple chunk... well, you're laughing.

Cheeky
Sweet & Sour Pork

Prepare in 25 mins · Cook in 45 mins · Serves 2-4

1 tbsp olive oil
500g lean pork, cut into 3cm cubes
2 tsp cornflour
227g can of pineapple chunks in juice
4 tbsp white wine vinegar
50g soft light brown sugar
1 tbsp light soya sauce
1 onion, thinly sliced
1 large carrot, peeled and cut into batons
1 yellow and 1 red pepper, deseeded and cut
   into strips
75g unsalted cashew nuts
small bunch of coriander, leaves picked

FOR THE RICE
olive oil
1 lemon, halved
240g long-grain or basmati rice
salt and pepper

Heat the oil in a large wok over a high heat and add the pork chunks. Stir-fry for 7–8 minutes until browned all over. Sift the cornflour over the pork, turning to coat, and set aside.

Drain the juice from the pineapple chunks into a measuring jug and add cold water

to make up to 250ml. Add this and the pineapple chunks to the browned pork and place over a medium heat. Stir in the vinegar, brown sugar and soya sauce and bring to the boil. Add the onion, carrot and peppers, reduce the heat and leave to simmer, uncovered, for 25 minutes.

Lightly toast the cashew nuts in a dry frying pan until golden and evenly coloured. Allow to cool. Set aside while you prepare the rice.

Bring a large pan of water to the boil, add a glug of olive oil, a lemon half and the rice. Reduce the heat and simmer for 8–10 minutes (check it a couple of times). When it is cooked but still erring on the nutty side, drain and then pour over some just-boiled water from the kettle to rinse away any excess starch. Return to the pan, squeeze over the other lemon half, add another glug of olive oil and salt and pepper to taste. Stir through.

Scatter the toasted cashews and coriander leaves over the pork and serve with the rice.

I often do these for footy-on-the-telly days or the Eurovision Song Contest. Finger food like this ensures that not a goal/song is missed (whether you like it or not). Plus a lot of sticky sauce on the faces of all the sitting-room pundits. Perfect.

My Mum's
Spare Ribs

Prepare in 10 mins · Cook in 1½ hours · Serves 4

1.2kg pork spare ribs (about 12)
6 tbsp dark soya sauce
3 tbsp honey or brown sugar
3 tbsp red or white wine vinegar
4–5 tbsp dry sherry
2 tbsp finely chopped fresh ginger

Place the ribs in a large pan – a stock pot would be ideal. Add the soya sauce and 600ml water – enough to just cover the ribs. Bring to the boil and skim off any scum that rises to the surface (sounds unpleasant, but be not alarmed). Reduce the heat and cook for 45 minutes to 1 hour, checking occasionally to skim off any further scum that appears.

Add the honey or sugar, vinegar, sherry and ginger and continue to cook, uncovered, for 20–30 minutes over a medium heat. Keep a close eye on the ribs and keep stirring them. The mixture will gradually reduce around the ribs to create a sticky wonderfulness. Just don't let the pan boil dry as I once did!

Serve straight from the pan, or tip onto a large dish and watch them miraculously become clean bones as everyone tucks in.

Another quick and really hearty tea. My boys are always pleased to see a schnitzel. I find the humble breadcrumb can really transport things. Bung some dried herbs in with them too if you are feeling perky. This is lovely with potato wedges, peas and ketchup, too.

Simple Pork Schnitzel

Prepare in 40 mins · Cook in 25 mins · Serves 4

4 pork escalopes, about 150g each,
   trimmed of fat
4 tbsp plain flour
2 eggs, beaten
100g fresh breadcrumbs
700g carrots, cut into batons
2 tbsp olive oil
30g butter

FOR THE CASHEW NUT PESTO
6 sun-dried tomatoes from a jar, drained
60g cashew nuts
50g finely grated Parmesan
1 small red pepper, deseeded and
   roughly chopped
1 garlic clove, crushed
50ml olive oil
salt and pepper

FOR THE BASIL RICE
200g basmati rice
25g bunch of basil, leaves only
1 tbsp olive oil
juice of ½ lemon

First make the pesto. Place the sun-dried tomatoes, cashew nuts, Parmesan, red pepper, garlic and some seasoning in a food processor and pulse to combine. Add the olive oil and pulse again until you have a lovely orangey paste.

Prepare the pork schnitzels by covering the escalopes with cling film or baking paper and bashing out each one on a board, using a meat mallet or rolling pin. Arrange your dipping ingredients in shallow bowls: flour in one, beaten eggs in another and breadcrumbs in another and lightly season each one. Dip each bashed escalope first in flour, then egg, then breadcrumbs and place on a tray until ready to cook.

Start cooking the rice in a large pan of boiling salted water. Keep checking the rice, but it should be ready after about 8–10 minutes. Steam or boil the carrots to your liking. Meanwhile blitz the basil leaves, olive oil and lemon juice to make a basil oil. Set aside.

Heat a large non-stick frying pan over a medium-high heat and add the oil and butter. Wait for it to stop sizzling and then add the schnitzels. Fry gently for 3–4 minutes on each side, until golden. Drain on kitchen paper.

Mix the basil oil through the drained rice. Toss the carrots in the cashew nut pesto. Use as much or as little as you like – any leftover pesto will keep for a good few days in the fridge and can be used for pasta, in wraps or drizzled over a bowl of soup, even. I like shaping the rice into mounds to serve – anything for a laugh.

Oh, I am partial to a bit of pork, it's true. It's such a generous meat with its crackling and its oh-so-many ways of being itself. From the humble banger to the proudest of glistening joints. Yes, we do love pig on a Sunday. Here's a version with some chestnut balls...

Pork Belly with Chestnut Balls

Prepare in 30 mins · Cook in 2–2½ hours · Serves 6

FOR THE PORK
6 small eating apples, peeled and cored
6 shallots, 3 left whole (unpeeled)
   and 3 peeled and chopped
small bunch of thyme, leaves picked
1 tbsp honey
1 tbsp aged balsamic vinegar
1kg piece of pork belly joint, skin scored
500ml good dry cider (the bottled variety)

FOR THE STUFFING BALLS
400g pork sausages
6 sage leaves, chopped
1 tbsp smoothish chutney
3–4 sun-dried tomatoes in oil, chopped
2 Medjool dates, de-stoned and chopped
1 heaped tsp Dijon mustard
40g vacuum-packed cooked chestnuts,
   crumbled
30g toasted pine nuts
1 tsp redcurrant jelly
1 large egg
80–100g breadcrumbs
salt and pepper

FOR THE VEGETABLES
400g bunched carrots, cleaned and
   trimmed but left whole
500g raw beetroot, peeled and cut into
   wedges
small handful of fresh oregano or thyme
1 tbsp honey
2 tbsp olive oil

splash of white wine
900g Desiree potatoes, peeled
   and cut into chunks
2 tbsp plain flour
2 tbsp olive oil
30g duck/goose fat
salt and pepper

FOR THE GRAVY
300ml chicken stock
1 tbsp cornflour

Preheat the oven to 180°C/160°C fan/Gas 4.

Arrange the apples and chopped and whole shallots in the base of a large roasting tin and scatter over the thyme leaves. Drizzle with the honey and balsamic vinegar. Nestle the pork joint on top and then pour the cider into the roasting tin (the cook may need a swig or two first) keeping the skin of the meat dry. Place in the oven for 2 hours.

Now for the stuffing. Take the sausages and squeeze the meat from their skins into a large bowl. Add all the remaining ingredients, adding just enough breadcrumbs so that the mixture is neither too wet nor too dry. Squidge together with your hands until well combined. Roll the mixture into 12–14 balls and place on an oiled baking tray (use some of the oil from the sun-dried tomatoes).

Put your carrots on one side of a roasting tin and the beetroot on the other. Add the fresh oregano or thyme and season with salt. Drizzle over the honey, olive oil and white wine.

Parboil the potatoes in boiling salted water for 10 minutes, drain and leave to steam dry in a colander. Tip into a roasting tin and sprinkle with the flour, olive oil, duck/goose fat and seasoning.

When the meat has been in the oven for about 1 hour, put your potatoes in. After 20 minutes or so add your vegetables and the stuffing balls. In short, the meat needs about 2 hours, the potatoes about 1 hour and the stuffing balls and vegetables about 40 minutes. Keep an eye on the various components and swap shelves or cover

with foil if anything looks like it might be browning too much.

Remove the pork roasting tin from the oven and transfer the pork joint to a separate baking tray. Increase the oven temperature to 220°C/200°C fan/Gas 7 and return the pork to the oven for a further 10–15 minutes to crisp up the skin. Meanwhile make the gravy. Remove the apples from the tin and add the chicken stock. Deglaze the pan over a medium heat and bubble for a minute or two. Mix the cornflour with a little of the hot liquid and then use the paste to thicken the gravy.

Everything you need for a fetching Sunday roast.

Mum always made a big ham for fireworks night. This was quite an event in our old house where we grew up, as we had a tiered garden so the people going 'ooh' and 'ahhhh' could stand safely at the bottom, and then there were steps up to where the display was. My dad was the head firework lighter, and always did slightly jokey delaying tactics to ratchet up the tension. I was a timid child and hid with our cat 'Boot' and Granny Annie upstairs (plus a plate of ham and a baked tattie, naturally).

Ginger Mango Gammon

Prepare in 25 mins · Cook in 3½ hours, plus cooling · Serves 12–15

3kg piece of smoked or unsmoked gammon, skin on
1.5 litre bottle of ginger beer
10cm piece of fresh ginger, thinly sliced
2 tsp ground ginger
2–3 litres water
20–30 cloves

FOR THE GLAZE
150g mango chutney
30g demerara sugar
1 tbsp dark soya sauce
2 tsp ground ginger

First of all calculate your cooking time. Weigh your gammon joint and allow 30 minutes per 500g. I've used a 3kg joint here so the cooking time will be 3 hours.

Pour the ginger beer into a very large pan or stock pot. Add the fresh and ground ginger and place the gammon carefully in the pan. Top up with the water until just covered. Place over a high heat and bring to the boil, skimming off any scum that appears on the surface. Lower the heat and leave to simmer for 3 hours (or more or less, depending on the size of your joint).

Turn off the heat and allow the gammon to cool in the liquid for a couple of hours – if you can – to really allow the flavours to infuse. Remove from the pan and set aside.

Meanwhile preheat the oven to 200°C/180°C fan/Gas 6. Prepare the glaze by mixing together all the glaze ingredients in a bowl.

When the gammon is cool enough to handle, remove the skin and cut away about half of the fat layer. Score the fat that is left on the ham in a criss-cross pattern, making diamond shapes. Stud each diamond with a clove and then spoon and spread the glaze all over the outside of the gammon. Place the joint in a roasting tin and roast for 20–30 minutes, until the joint is gloriously golden and caramelised all over. If serving hot, leave to rest for 10 minutes before carving.

Beautiful cut cold with a pickled onion and a hunk of bread. Or just a hunk.

The boys love these. They say they are more mysterious than a pizza. When they were littler we were forever assembling pizzas and sprinkling toppings here, there and everywhere. Literally. You can't argue with a pizza. Well, you could but I'd hazard the pizza would win.

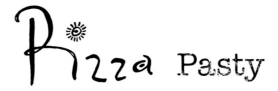

Pizza Pasty

Prepare in 20 mins, plus proving · Cook in 20 mins · Serves 2

FOR THE BASE
250g strong white bread flour
½ tsp salt
½ sachet (7g) fast-action dried yeast
1 tbsp olive oil, plus extra for greasing
about 160ml warm water

FOR THE TOPPING
6 tbsp Tomato Sauce (see page 95)
few fresh basil leaves
about 12 black olives
6–8 slices of salami
150g ball of mozzarella, torn into chunks
handful of grated Cheddar

Sift the flour into a large bowl and mix in the salt. Mix the dried yeast, olive oil and water together in a jug and then add to the flour. Mix well with your hands. Start kneading – it will need a good 10 minutes by hand. You can, of course, do this in a food mixer with a dough hook attachment, if you have one.

When you have a nice smooth dough put it in a lightly oiled bowl, cover with cling film and leave to prove: for 1 hour in a warm place or 2 hours at room temperature. While the dough is proving, prepare your

trusty tomato sauce and toppings, adding the basil leaves to the tomato sauce. Preheat the oven to 200°C/180°C fan/Gas 6 and put a large flat baking tray in the oven.

Turn your risen dough out on to a lightly oiled surface and knead for a few minutes. Halve the dough and shape each piece into a circle, stretching it out with your hands (you are looking for a nice thin circle, about 28cm in diameter). Spread the tomato sauce over one half of each circle and then scatter your chosen toppings over the sauce. Fold the pizza in half and seal with your fingers – like a pasty (the proper name for this is calzone).

Transfer your pizza pasties to your preheated tray and cook in the oven for 20 minutes, until golden.

I absolutely love venison but my boys aren't mad for it, so I don't cook it as often as I'd like to. I used to have an allotment with a glut of blackberries, hence the choice of gravy. If venison is ever on the menu in a restaurant I will invariably plump for it. It is full of flavour and very lean, too, so it also feels like a healthy option. It's win-win with game!

Venison with Blackberry gravy

Prepare in 20 mins · Cook in 1 hour · Serves 4

FOR THE BLACKBERRY GRAVY
1 tbsp aged balsamic vinegar
250ml beef stock
1–2 tbsp rowan or redcurrant jelly
2 garlic cloves, crushed
200g blackberries
175ml red wine

FOR THE VEGETABLES
4 medium parsnips, peeled and
  cut into chunks
1 chicken or vegetable stock cube
30g butter
1 tsp cumin seeds
500g Brussels sprouts, peeled and trimmed
salt and pepper

FOR THE VENISON
600g piece of venison tenderloin
1 tbsp oil
1 tbsp butter, plus extra to finish the gravy
1 tbsp freshly chopped parsley

First of all make the blackberry gravy. Put all the gravy ingredients in a large, heavy-based pan and bring to a gentle simmer. I use rowan jelly because my mum makes it and I love its beautiful colour and flavour, but redcurrant makes a perfectly good substitute. Cook for about 20 minutes until reduced and the blackberries are soft, and then press through a sieve into a clean pan. Continue to reduce the sauce for about 5 minutes, tasting as you go. It should have a lovely sweet and sour tang, so add more jelly if you think it needs it. Set aside.

Take the meat out of the fridge 30 minutes before cooking and pat dry with kitchen paper.

Place the parsnips and stock cube in a large pan of water and bring to the boil. Simmer for about 15 minutes until good and tender, then drain and mash, adding about half the butter and some seasoning. Toast the cumin seeds in a dry frying pan, crush lightly and stir into your mash. Keep warm.

Put your Brussels on to boil or steam for around 8–10 minutes. Meanwhile start cooking the venison. Heat the oil and butter in a large frying pan until it stops sizzling. Season the venison all over and then add to the hot pan. Cook for about 4–6 minutes on each side over a medium-high heat until nicely caramelised on the outside. Venison is best served rare to medium; I'm a medium gal so I go for about 6 minutes. Baste the loin occasionally with the oil and butter. Remove from the pan and transfer to a plate to rest for a few minutes, covered with foil.

Drain the sprouts and toss in the remaining butter with some salt and pepper. Reheat the gravy, whisking a wee knob of butter into it to add a bit of shine. Slice the venison and assemble all the characters in your venison story on a lovely plate that will do your efforts justice. Scatter with parsley and serve with the gravy and vegetables.

Vegetabley things

I was a vegetarian for years, from my student days in Bristol to when I was working in Stratford at the Royal Shakespeare Company trying desperately to make sense of The Bard. Then someone broke my heart a bit, and I rebounded straight into a beef and horseradish sandwich. Two in a row. On the Finchley Road. Red-eyed and ravenous. My vegetarian days were over. This recipe, however, was always my favourite veggie option.

Melanzane

Prepare in 20 mins · Cook in 1 hour · Serves 4

FOR THE TOMATO SAUCE
1 tbsp olive oil
1 onion, finely chopped
3 garlic cloves
1.2kg ripe tomatoes, skinned (see page 59)
  and chopped
1 tbsp aged balsamic vinegar
1 tsp brown sugar
salt and pepper

2 large aubergines, sliced,
  about 5mm thick
good-quality olive oil, for brushing
100g Parmesan, finely grated
2 x 125g balls of mozzarella, torn into
  chunks
handful of fresh basil leaves
75g fresh breadcrumbs

First make your tomato sauce. Heat the oil in a large pan and add the onion. Soften over a medium heat for about 5 minutes, then add the garlic and cook for a few more minutes. Add the chopped tomatoes, balsamic vinegar, sugar and salt and pepper and bring to a simmer. Let it bubble away on a low heat for about 20 minutes until thick and reduced.

Preheat the oven to 200°C/180°C fan/Gas 6.

Place a griddle pan over a medium-high heat, and dry griddle your aubergine slices in batches until slightly charred on both sides. Set aside and drizzle lightly with your best olive oil.

Start assembling your melanzane in an ovenproof dish. Spread a layer of tomato sauce over the base and top with a couple of tablespoons of grated Parmesan, some torn mozzarella and a few basil leaves. Add a layer of aubergine slices and then repeat twice, so you have three good layers, ending with a layer of tomato sauce. Reserve 2 tablespoons of Parmesan and a few torn basil leaves and mix with the breadcrumbs for the topping.

Bake in the oven for about 20 minutes. Remove from the oven and scatter over the breadcrumb mixture. Return to the oven for a further 10 minutes.

Richard and I were always a bit too scared to do risotto. We both had in our heads that it was very difficult. Then one day we did it; it wasn't – and we are utter risotto converts. Mushroom and pea is our favourite. The boys don't like it yet – all the more for us!

This is a great supper dish if you're catering for a mix of meat-eaters and veggies as, despite having no meat, it's very filling and seems to satisfy all appetites. Just serve up with a crunchy salad.

Wild Mushroom & Pea
Risotto

Prepare in 10 mins · Cook in 50 mins · Serves 6

100g butter
225g chestnut mushrooms, sliced
225g wild mushrooms, wiped and roughly torn or sliced
1 tbsp olive oil
1 red onion, finely chopped
2 garlic cloves, finely chopped
650g Arborio rice
1.5 litres chicken stock (or vegetable if veggies are present)
400ml dry white wine
300–400g frozen peas, defrosted
200g grated Parmesan
salt and pepper

Melt about 25g of the butter in a large frying pan and add all your mushrooms. Season with salt and pepper and cook gently for a few minutes until softened. Set aside.

Heat another 25g of butter and the olive oil in a large pan over a low-medium heat and add the chopped onion. Soften gently for about 6–8 minutes and then add the garlic. When the onion and garlic is soft and translucent, but not coloured, add the rice and stir until the grains are coated in the lovely, buttery onion.

Start adding the chicken stock gradually, stirring well after each ladle. After a few ladles alternate stock with wine. It can be difficult to quantify exactly how much liquid you need, as every risotto is different, so it's best to have plenty of good stock to hand. Just keep adding the liquid, a ladleful at a time, and stir well until it's quietly absorbed. Check the rice to see if it is cooked; when you reach a good consistency stir in the fried mushrooms and peas. Taste and adjust the seasoning.

Just before serving stir in the grated Parmesan and remaining butter. Serve hot from the pot – bliss-o.

My amazing pal Tam has had two brilliant pub restaurants:
the Engineer in Primrose Hill and the Hampshire Hog in Hammersmith.
My rare treat is to meet her for lunch and try out the new things
on a menu. Such a chore. Tam is also a psychotherapist.
I think that can only help in a kitchen.

Tam's Coconut Lentil Dahl

Prepare in 25 mins · Cook in 45 mins · Serves 4

generous knob of butter
1 tbsp vegetable oil
2 medium onions, chopped
1 tsp ground turmeric
2 garlic cloves, crushed
large thumb-sized piece of fresh ginger,
    peeled and finely chopped
1 large red chilli, deseeded and finely
    chopped
250g dried red lentils
400ml can coconut milk
300–450ml chicken or vegetable stock
juice of 1 lime
handful of coriander leaves
salt and pepper

Heat the butter and oil in a large pan over a low heat. Add the onions and cook until softened and golden, about 15 minutes. Stir in the turmeric (marvel at the beautiful colour if you're in the mood) and then add the garlic, ginger and chilli and cook for 2 minutes, stirring.

Add the lentils, coconut milk and 300ml of the stock. Bring to a simmer and continue to cook gently, partially covered, for about 30 minutes. The dahl will thicken as it cooks, so if you like a slightly looser dahl, add more stock. (At this point you could turn the dahl into a soup by adding more stock and whizzing to a smooth consistency. Fabulous.)

Squeeze over the lime juice and then taste and adjust the seasoning. Serve scattered with fresh coriander leaves – on its own, with some plain boiled rice, or as a heavenly side for any curry.

ooh I doo luvva lentil

Where we live, we happen to be flanked on both sides by the Kapoors and the Parson Kapoors. Neighbour-wise we completely lucked out. Plus the cooking... Oh my. The spices, the fragrance, the beauty of it all. When we pop over for supper we are very happy on every level. The roll home is the cherry. This little beauty is thanks to Chander Veer Kapoor.

Chander Kapoor's
Awesome Aubergines

Prepare in 10 mins, plus marinating · Cook in 45 mins · Serves 4 as a side

12 baby aubergines
1 tbsp vegetable oil
3–4 onions, thinly sliced

FOR THE SPICE MIX
¾ tsp ground turmeric
¾ tsp salt
¾ tsp ground cumin
¾ tsp ground coriander
¾ tsp garam masala
¼–½ tsp chilli powder
1–2 tsp dried mango powder (amchoor)
½ tsp ground ginger
2–3 tbsp vegetable oil

Take your aubergines and cut them lengthways into quarters from bottom to stem, taking care not to cut through the stem.

Mix together all the ingredients for the spice mix in a large bowl and use to slather your aubergines inside and out. Leave to marinate while you get on with the rest of the recipe.

Heat the oil in a large frying pan with a lid (I use a lidded wok) and add the sliced onions. Cook over a medium heat for about 8–10 minutes, until softened. Add the marinated aubergines, cover and cook over a low-medium heat until the onions have turned caramelly and the aubergines are cooked through and slightly roasted, about 20–25 minutes. Turn them gently from time to time.

It really is worth seeking out the little baby aubergines for this dish – most Asian/Indian supermarkets have them. You will find amchoor there too. It was a revelation to me!

When I found out I was going to do *MasterChef*, Dan and Martha
at Franco's of Friern Barnet (our favourite Italian restaurant),
welcomed me into their kitchen for some practising. They even set up
a *MasterChef* 'box test' for me. It was brilliant. I seem to remember
I did a little guinea fowl with herbs (never done that before!) and
a rhubarb crème brûlée that didn't set. Martha's did.

Martha & Dan's
Napoli Peppers

Prepare in 15 mins · Cook in 40 mins · Serves 4

2 tbsp olive oil
2 garlic cloves, crushed
12 black olives, pitted
2 tsp capers
2 red peppers, halved and deseeded
8 anchovy fillets in oil, drained
50g finely grated Parmesan

FOR THE TOMATO SAUCE
400g can chopped tomatoes
1 tsp dried oregano
1 tsp brown sugar
salt and pepper

First make the tomato sauce. Put the
chopped tomatoes, oregano, sugar and
seasoning in a pan and bubble together
over a medium heat for about 15 minutes
to reduce slightly. Set aside. Alternatively
use the Tomato Sauce on page 95.

Preheat the oven to 180°C/160°C fan/Gas 4.

Heat the olive oil in a large frying pan over
a medium heat. Stir in the garlic, olives and
capers and cook for 2–3 minutes. Add the
tomato sauce (about 6 ladles) and simmer
for about 5 minutes.

Place the red pepper halves in a lightly
oiled roasting tin or oven dish and divide
the sauce between them. Press 2 anchovy
fillets into each one and sprinkle over the
Parmesan cheese. Bake in the oven for
20–30 minutes.

Lovely as a starter but also lip-smacking
with both meat and fish dishes.

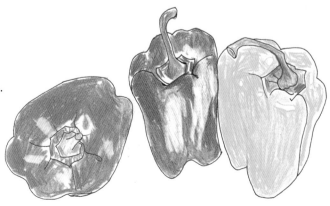

This is such a simple way to cook our humble potato, but it always looks
so appealing and feels rather unusual. A great accompaniment
to so many things, and another good reason to have a
pot of stock on the go whenever possible.

Herby Boulangère Potatoes

Prepare in 10 mins · Cook in 30–40 mins · Serves 4 as a side

olive oil, for greasing
2 large Desiree potatoes, thinly sliced
  (leave them unpeeled)
1 red onion, thinly sliced
1 white onion, thinly sliced
1 tbsp fresh oregano or thyme,
  or 1 tsp dried
400ml good chicken stock
generous knob of butter
salt and pepper

Preheat the oven to 180°C/160°C fan/Gas 4 and lightly oil a suitable baking dish – I use an old enamel dish, about 22 x 22cm, that looks very lovely just plonked on the table – a random dish can be an inspiring thing!

Layer your sliced potatoes and onions in the dish, adding salt and pepper as you go and sprinkling with herbs. Pour the chicken stock over the top and bake in the oven for about 30–40 minutes. Towards the end of the cooking time, dot the top of the potatoes with butter to help the potatoes brown – who doesn't like a bit of butter on their taytoes?

This is a simple celebration of the turnip, a vegetable that could do with a bit more attention, I'd say. The parsnip, for instance, gets a lot of job opportunities in comparison. Well, I think the turnip is beautiful, (I want to paint it, let alone eat it!) but also really tasty and surprising. This is an old Scottish recipe.

Clapshot

Prepare in 10 mins · Cook in 20 mins · Serves 4 as a side

1 tbsp vegetable bouillon powder
2 turnips, peeled and chopped
2 large potatoes, peeled and chopped
60g butter
salt and pepper

Bring a large pan of water to the boil and add the bouillon powder. Add the turnips and potatoes and cook until soft, about 15 minutes.

Drain in a colander and steam dry for a few minutes before mashing. I like a rough mash on this one, but it's all down to personal preference. Add the butter and lots of salt and pepper and serve – it's a winner with meat or fish.

Richard is 'Salad King' in our house – he just always manages to make them taste utterly the best. His secret ingredient is often sunflower seeds, which he roasts in a little pan with some soya sauce (the secret is out!). They seem to go with everything and the salty nuttiness is gorgeous. I've suggested a tahini dressing here, but you could also try this with Duck Poo Dressing (see page 143).

Asparagus, Chicory &
Pomegranate Salad

Prepare in 10 mins · Cook in 20 mins · Serves 2 as a main, 4 as a side

large bunch (350g) asparagus
2 tsp olive oil
2 tsp aged balsamic vinegar
juice of ½ lemon
seeds of ½ pomegranate
100g mixed salad leaves
1 head of chicory, leaves separated
200g feta cheese, crumbled
handful of sunflower seeds
1 tsp soya sauce
salt and pepper

FOR THE TAHINI DRESSING
2 tsp tahini
juice of ½ lemon
juice of ½ orange
1 garlic clove, crushed
2 tsp olive oil

Preheat the oven to 180°C/160°C fan/Gas 4.

Snap the woody ends off the asparagus and then slice each spear in half lengthways. Place in a roasting tray in a single layer and drizzle over the olive oil, balsamic vinegar and lemon juice. Season with salt and pepper and roast in the oven for about 20 minutes, or until tender.

Meanwhile, prepare the pomegranate. Hold one half over a bowl and use a rolling pin to gently bash the pomegranate skin. The gorgeous pink seeds should start working their way out. Keep at it, massaging the pomegranate to release the seeds as you go.

Put the salad and chicory leaves in a serving bowl or on a big plate and toss through the pomegranate seeds. Stir through your lovely roasted asparagus and crumbled feta. Toast the sunflower seeds in a dry frying pan for a few minutes and, as they start to turn brown, add the soya sauce and sizzle for 20 seconds. Throw into your salad.

To make the tahini dressing, whisk together all the ingredients in a small bowl (or shake in a jar with a tight-fitting lid). Drizzle over your salad and serve.

I sometimes go a bit blank when it comes to salads. I think it's partly because Richard is so good at them, and I often leave them to him. That said, inspiration occasionally strikes. I love watercress and I love prunes and I thought they might love each other. I think they do.

This one goes nicely with the Salmon and Dill Fishcakes (see page 55).

Watercress & Prune Salad

Prepare in 5 mins · Cook in 15 mins · Serves 4

handful of walnuts, broken into pieces
100g watercress
1 small cooked beetroot, peeled and sliced
    into matchsticks
½ fennel bulb, finely sliced
handful of pitted prunes, sliced

FOR THE TAHINI CITRUS DRESSING
3 tsp tahini
juice of ½ orange
juice of ½ lemon
2–3 tbsp extra-virgin olive oil
1 tsp runny honey
1 tsp garlic paste (from a tube)
salt and pepper

Preheat the oven to 180°C/160°C fan/Gas 4.

Tip the walnuts on to a baking tray and roast in the oven for about 10 minutes, checking and shaking them halfway through cooking, until they start to release their oils.

Put all the dressing ingredients into a jar with a tight-fitting lid and shake to combine.

Arrange the watercress, beetroot, fennel and prunes on a serving plate and top with the roasted walnuts. Drizzle over the dressing and serve.

Love triumphs.

These are a great veggie side, or something to use as a starter with smoked salmon, cream cheese and lots of cracked pepper aloft. Cheap, quick, easy... I'll stop talking about myself now.

Courgette &
Parmesan Patties

Prepare in 10 mins · Cook in 10 mins · Makes about 10

2 large courgettes
2 large eggs, beaten
150g plain flour
60g melted butter
100g grated Parmesan
1 tsp celery salt
black pepper
vegetable oil, for frying

Grate the courgettes coarsely and then squeeze handfuls of the grated courgette in kitchen paper, to remove any excess water. Place the squeezed courgette in a large bowl.

Add the eggs, flour, melted butter, Parmesan, celery salt and pepper and mix well to combine, using your hands if you feel like it.

Put a couple of tablespoons of vegetable oil in a non-stick frying pan and place over a medium heat. Use a spoon to put large blobs of courgette mixture into the pan and flatten slightly into patty shapes. Cook in batches, taking care not to overcrowd the pan, for about 5 minutes on each side. Drain on kitchen paper and keep warm in a low oven if necessary.

I'm partial to a bit of coleslaw — even that stuff that you could use as all-over body moisturiser occasionally draws me. This is a great alternative for adding colour to any dish; it goes brilliantly with the Saucy Barbecue Chicken on page 72.

Blue Cheese
Coleslaw

Prepare in 20 mins · Serves 8

FOR THE GARLIC MAYONNAISE
2 large egg yolks
1 tsp garlic paste or ½ garlic clove, crushed
1 tsp white wine vinegar
½ tsp Dijon mustard
150ml olive oil
salt and pepper

FOR THE COLESLAW
300g (about ½) red cabbage, cored
    and finely sliced
300g (about ½) white cabbage, cored
    and finely sliced
2 large carrots, coarsely grated
½ fennel bulb, finely sliced
50g golden raisins
1 tsp fresh thyme leaves
100g Stilton, crumbled

Start by making the mayonnaise. Place the egg yolks in a large bowl with the garlic, wine vinegar and mustard and whisk together until combined. Start to add the oil, literally a drop at a time, while still whisking so that it emulsifies slowly. Gradually increase the amount of oil you add to a slow drizzle, whisking or beating all the time. Once all the oil has been added, taste and adjust the seasoning.

In a separate bowl mix together the cabbages, carrot, fennel, raisins, thyme leaves and Stilton. Spoon over the mayonnaise and stir until well combined. Chill until ready to serve.

This was named by my mum, so don't blame me. A sweet, rich and simple dressing – almost a dip – to drip over any salad or even just a plain avocado. I sometimes spread it on toast... is that wrong?

Mum's Duck Poo
Dressing

Prepare in 5 mins · Makes about 8 tablespoons

1 tsp muscovado sugar
1 large garlic clove, crushed
1 tsp grainy mustard
1 tsp balsamic vinegar
juice of ½ lemon
4–5 tbsp good olive oil
salt and pepper

Put the sugar, garlic, mustard, vinegar, lemon juice and salt and pepper in a bowl and whisk together to combine.

Continue to whisk or stir while very slowly drizzling in your favourite olive oil. Keep whisking, as if you were making mayonnaise, until it looks glossy and has a nice thick consistency. Taste and adjust the seasoning, adding a little more of whatever you think it needs.

Lovely with any salad.

I got the gist of this from a Women's Institute recipe my mother-in-law Anne gave me. I added the carrots and red pepper, as I love the colours and different textures. If you ever come across romanesco cauliflower do use it here; its psychedelic green colour and pointy appearance make it worth seeking out. Piccalilli has such a beautiful hue in the kitchen and the name alone makes it worth making. Even if you don't like it, there's something intrinsically amusing about Piccalilli.

Piccalilli

Prepare in 50 mins · Cook in 30 minutes, plus cooling and maturing · Makes 10 jars

1 large cauliflower (about 1.2kg), cut into tiny florets
450g pickling onions or small shallots, finely chopped
1.25 litres distilled white malt vinegar
3 carrots, cut into 1–2cm pieces
150g green beans, cut into 1–2cm lengths
2 courgettes, soft middle removed and cut into 1–2cm pieces
2 large garlic cloves, finely chopped
450g caster sugar
50g dry mustard powder
115g plain flour
25g ground turmeric
1 tsp ground coriander
2 tsp fine salt
1 red pepper, deseeded and cut into 1–2cm pieces

First sterilise your jars. Preheat the oven to 140°C/120°C fan/Gas 1. Wash your jars thoroughly in hot soapy water and rinse well. Place the jars and lids directly on the oven shelf, upside down, and leave in the oven for 15 minutes.

Place the cauliflower florets in a very large pan or preserving pan and add the onions or shallots and 1 litre of the vinegar. Bring to the boil and simmer for 10 minutes.

Add the carrots, green beans and courgettes (you need about 900g mixed vegetables in total) along with the garlic and sugar. Bring back to a simmer and cook for a further 10 minutes.

Meanwhile mix together the mustard powder, flour, turmeric, ground coriander, salt and remaining vinegar in a bowl to make a lovely vivid coloured paste. Add this to the pan of vegetables along with the chopped red pepper and whisk in so there are no lumps. Continue to cook for another 10 minutes. Remove from the heat and allow to cool before spooning into your sterilised jars.

Let the piccalilli mature for at least 2–3 weeks before using. It will keep unopened for 12–18 months. Once opened, store in the fridge.

CHOC POTS

melt 150
~~200~~ g choc various
~~50~~ — ~~marshers~~ marshers

tsp vanilla
75 boiling water
100 double cream

Pure Rich Cream

LANC:
Yeah?

ANDY
Yeah. They're pac
Homeward bound.

They touch fists.
Andy passes back the bins.

LANC:
Bishop's down the

ANDY
Is he?

LANC:
We should get dow
what's afoot. May
sweep of that spo

ANDY
Have you got your

LANC:

6 oz. shredded
12 oz demerara
½ lb. sultanas
1 lb. Bramle
½ lb. currans
12 oz. stoned r
½ lb. cut mixed
1 lemon rind
1 lime rind or

Sugar

Jam &
Suzn
Jam
Rotem
Pistachios
Ricotta.

Coffee Mallow.

12 or so marshmallows.
melted in cup of hot coffee
cool & when beginning to
stir in cup whipped cream.
¼ teasp. vanilla.

Who's 4 Pud?

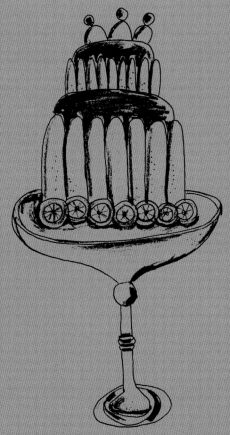

I think in a recipe book it's probably wise to avoid talking about religion, politics and education – best just to stick to the staff of life...
But why should Eton have all the fun? Let's redress the balance!

State Skool
Mess

Prepare in 10 mins · Cook in 5 mins · Serves 4

500ml vanilla ice cream (the best quality you can muster)
1 Curly Wurly, snipped into pieces
2 funsize Milky Ways, chopped
1 Crunchie, chopped
1 Jammy Dodger, chopped
1 pink and 1 purple Party Ring, broken into pieces (I know, I'm stipulating colour – it's madness)
2 Mars bars, roughly chopped
splash of milk (optional)
150g raspberries

Take the ice cream out of the freezer and leave to soften just enough so that it becomes stirrable. Scoop the lot into a large mixing bowl and add the Curly Wurly, Milky Ways, Crunchie, Jammy Dodger and Party Rings. Stir until it is all mixed together and then spoon back into your ice cream carton (curiously, you will find that it does fit back in).

When you are ready to serve, melt the Mars bars in a bain-marie (a heatproof bowl set over a pan of just-simmering water). If a bain-marie feels like too much effort, just melt in a pan over a very low heat with a splash of milk – this will take about 5 minutes.

Scoop your customized ice cream into bowls, pour over your Mars bar sauce and scatter a few raspberries over the whole shebang.

Up the revolution!

I do love a passion fruit. It has got to be one of the most magical fruit flavours. (I'd like to create a passion fruit perfume.) The seeds, though, are a caution, I find. Problem solved in the Passion Fruit Pot. Thank you, Steve the Sieve.

Passion Pots

Prepare in 20 mins, plus cooling and chilling · Cook in 10 mins · Serves 2

2 gelatine leaves
6 ripe passion fruits
3 tbsp caster sugar
150ml double cream
mint sprigs, to serve

FOR THE HAZELNUT TOPPING
40g hazelnuts
2 tsp granulated sugar

Place the gelatine leaves in a small bowl of cold water and set aside for about 5 minutes to soften.

Cut each passion fruit in half and scoop the insides into a small pan. Add the sugar and 180ml water. Place over a low heat and stir, squidging the seeds against the side of the pan with a wooden spoon to get as much of the soft flesh away from the seeds as possible. As soon as the sugar has dissolved, remove from the heat and strain the mixture through a sieve, pressing the pulp and seeds with the back of a spoon to get them to surrender their fruitiness.

Discard the pulp and seeds and tip the strained passion fruit liquid back into the pan. Place over a low heat. Squeeze the soaked gelatine leaves gently and add to the pan. Stir until it melts, then remove from the heat and allow to cool.

Once cooled, stir in the double cream and pour into four small dessert glasses or ramekins. Place in the fridge to set (at least 4 hours, or overnight).

To make the hazelnut topping, pulse the hazelnuts in a food processor until you have a nutty gravel (or just bash them in a bag with a rolling pin). Transfer to a small frying pan and add the sugar. Shake and swirl the pan over a medium heat until the sugar starts to melt and coat the hazelnut pieces; this should take about 6 minutes. When it looks the right shade of caramel, tip on to a plate to cool.

To serve, sprinkle the hazelnut topping over each passion fruit pot and decorate with a mint sprig.

Helloooo!

My Granny Megsie used to make this with the awesome Scottish raspberries that they grew underneath a big net in their garden. I loved being under that big netty thing, picking fruits and eating them and listening to bees humming in their huge fuchsia hedge.

Raspberry & Ginger
Shortbread Crumble

Prepare in 5 mins · Cook in 25 mins · Serves 4–6

500g raspberries
1–2 tbsp caster sugar
200g plain flour
150g butter, diced
75g granulated sugar
2 tsp ground ginger
2 tbsp crystallised ginger (optional), chopped
ice cream or Greek yogurt, to serve

Preheat the oven to 190°C/170°C fan/Gas 5.

Put your raspberries in the base of a shallow baking dish, about 20cm square. Sprinkle over the caster sugar – you may not need it all if your raspberries are nice and sweet.

In a separate bowl, rub together the flour and diced butter until you have a breadcrumb-like mixture. Stir in the granulated sugar, ground ginger and chopped crystallised ginger, if using. I do like this crumble quite gingery and it's such a great companion flavour to the raspberries.

Spread all this mixture over your raspberries and bake in the oven for 25 minutes. Serve warm with Greek yogurt or vanilla ice cream. Or chocolate ice cream. Okay, any ice cream.

Scottish Raspberries

There's a plethora of chocolate pots out there – lucky us. This is just a twist on an old favourite, guest-starring the magnificent Malteser. A treat of a pud that you can make in two shakes of a lamb's tail.

Malteser

Chocolate Pots

Prepare in 5 mins, plus chilling · Cook in 15 mins · Serves 4

**150g chocolate – use a mixture of
   dark and white, or whatever you
   have in your cupboard**
50g Maltesers
1 tsp vanilla extract
40ml boiling water
100ml double cream

First melt the chocolate in a bain-marie. Break the chocolate into pieces and put in a small heatproof bowl with the Maltesers. Place the bowl over a pan of barely simmering water, making sure that the base of the bowl does not touch the water.

Once the chocolate has melted, remove from the heat and give the chocolate a good stir, bashing the biscuity centres of the Maltesers so they are mixed in. Add the vanilla extract and the boiling water, a little at a time. Finally whisk in the cream. Divide the mixture equally between four little pots or ramekins and chill in the fridge for several hours before serving.

Take a seat, lick out the bowl and praise the corking cocoa bean.

This is a variation on a recipe I got from my mum. She didn't add gelatine. But when I tried her recipe it didn't set. She must have used a magic spell... I've used gelatine.

Coffee Mallow
Mousses

Prepare in 15 mins, plus chilling · Cook in 5 mins · Serves 6

2 gelatine leaves
400ml freshly made strong coffee
300g marshmallows (about 40 large)
300ml double cream
2 chocolate Flakes

Place the gelatine leaves in a small bowl of cold water and set aside for about 5 minutes to soften.

Pour the coffee into a large pan and add the marshmallows. Place over a medium heat and stir continuously – the mixture will bubble up, so beware! When the marshmallows have all melted, remove from the heat and set aside.

Squeeze the soaked gelatine leaves gently and add to the coffee and marshmallow mixture. Mix well until the gelatine has dissolved and set aside to cool.

Whip the double cream in a large bowl until soft peaks form. Pour the cooled coffee mixture into the cream and gently fold until combined. Pour into six individual ramekins and chill in the fridge for at least 4 hours or overnight.

Just before serving, cut the Flakes lengthways into chocolate shards and use to decorate these dreamy scamps.

I remember serving this up in Uncle James's café when I was a little girl. He served it with a big dollop of whipped cream that came out of a funny machine that you had to put a little gas canister into, like a SodaStream. It made the cream puff up like a Mr Whippy. I loved pushing down on the lever and making a bigger pile of cream than was respectable. I have no idea why it is Bavarian. It just makes it sound so unique. I don't think he ever went to Bavaria, but we all have our secrets.

Uncle James's
Bavarian Orange Pie

Prepare in 30 mins, plus chilling · Cook in 5 mins · Serves 8–10

FOR THE BASE
175g butter
225g digestive biscuits
175g soft light brown sugar

FOR THE TOPPING
350g white marshmallows
140ml freshly squeezed orange juice
zest of 1 orange
280ml double cream
½ tsp rosewater (optional)
3 large egg whites
handful of shelled unsalted pistachio nuts,
chopped

Melt the butter in a large pan. Blitz the biscuits to fine crumbs – either in a food processor or by placing them in a plastic bag and bashing them with a rolling pin. Add to the melted butter along with the sugar and stir well. Tip the mixture into a loose-bottomed 23cm fluted tart tin and press into the sides. Chill in the fridge for at least 30 minutes.

Meanwhile, place the marshmallows and orange juice in a large pan and stir over a medium heat until melted. Add the orange zest and then pour into a bowl and leave to cool to room temperature.

Using an electric whisk, whip the cream until soft peaks form, add rosewater (if using). Wash and dry the whisk attachments and then whisk the egg whites in a separate bowl until soft peaks form.

Fold the cream into the orange mixture and then gently fold in the whisked egg whites. Spoon over the biscuit base and then return to the fridge to set for at least 4 hours. Take out of the fridge a little while before removing from tin.

Just before serving, decorate with the pistachio nuts.

My Granny Megsie used to make several versions of this creamy dessert.
She called them 'Whim Whams for a Goose's Bridal'. (I know, odd.)
Here is the orange one, which was my favourite. The lemon version
is exactly the same, just using lemons instead of oranges.
This is a lovely thing to serve with an orange cake or
a lemony polenta cake (see page 164).
Just add a big blob on the side...

Megsie's Whim Whams

Prepare in 15 mins · Cook in 12 mins · Serves 4

**juice of 3 oranges, plus the finely
grated zest of 2 of them**
3 large eggs
300ml double cream
60g caster sugar
1 tsp orange flower water (optional)
30g soft butter

Put the orange juice, eggs, cream, caster
sugar and orange flower water, if using, in
a heatproof glass or metal bowl. Place the
bowl over a pan of barely simmering water,
making sure that the bottom of the bowl
doesn't touch the water. Using a balloon
whisk, mix together continuously until it
thickens. This will take anything from 8–12
minutes. Don't let the mixture boil or you'll
end up with scrambled eggs. As soon as the
mixture coats the back of a spoon, remove
from the heat and set aside to cool slightly.

While the custard is still just warm,
whisk in the butter and grated orange zest,
reserving a little of the zest to decorate.
Pour into four individual dessert glasses
or ramekins and top with the remaining
zest. Chill in the fridge for at least 4 hours,
or overnight.

Serve on its own, with cake or fresh fruit
such as strawberries.

Thank you, amazing Megsie, you and your
Whim Whams are the stuff of legend.

My oldest pal is called Susannah, but I have always called her Suki. We met when we were babies, as our parents were friends, having met in the 1950s in the West of England Theatre Company, touring together in rickety buses and putting up their own sets. Ooh, the smell of the grease paint, I love it!

Suki is an amazing cook AND baker. She has even made wedding cakes, and she is one of the most original women I know. One of my earliest memories is breaking the TV at her house, and hiding in a cupboard, and her dad, Michael, coaxing me out and promising that no one was cross. Also her mum, Rose, made the best sandwiches. White bread and everything. We never had white bread, as Mum was a bit brown ricey. This is a version of Suki's wonderful tiramisu.

Prepare in 30 mins, plus chilling · Serves 8–10

500g mascarpone
1–2 tbsp rum or brandy (I use both...
  is that wrong?)
4 eggs, separated
100g caster sugar
275ml strong black coffee (espresso
  strength)
150g sponge fingers
75g dark chocolate, fridge temperature
175g amaretti biscuits

Tip your mascarpone into a large bowl and allow to come to room temperature before beating with a wooden spoon to soften. Add the rum or brandy and mix until combined.

In a separate bowl, beat together the egg yolks and sugar until pale and creamy, then fold into the boozy mascarpone. In another clean bowl whisk the egg whites until stiff peaks form (an electric whisk is useful here) and fold them in too.

Pour your cooled coffee into a shallow dish. You can add a bit more alcohol to this if you like your tiramisuki a bit stronger! Turn the sponge fingers in the coffee puddle so they soak up some of the coffee and start lining your chosen dish, about 20 x 30cm and quite deepish. A glass or Pyrex dish is ideal as you can see the lovely layers.

Once you have your layer of soaked sponge fingers, spoon over about half the mascarpone mixture and spread so it is even. Generously grate over about half the chilled chocolate. Repeat this fragrant process with the amaretti biscuits, first soaking them in the coffee. You can, of course, go for more layers, depending on the size of your dish – just make sure you always finish with mascarpone and then grated chocolate.

Cover with cling film and chill in the fridge until needed. I find this works well if you make it several hours ahead so the flavours have a chance to meld together. Suki freezes hers, as she says it makes the flavours meld together best. She says it takes a day to thaw out at room temperature.

This is an old recipe that I've tinkered with, and it somehow treads the line between cooking and baking. I must admit when I last gave it a go, I so enjoyed it that I thought if it all dries up on the day/night job, I'll go into cheesecake production. I opted for a plum topping, as they were in season at the time and they have that edge that sets off the creamy cheesiness so well. But there are so many options: cherries, figs, raspberries, blueberries, to name but four.

Maple Syrup & Plum Cheesecake

Prepare in 20 mins, plus cooling and chilling · Cook in 1–1¼ hours · Serves 8–10

250g ginger nut biscuits
90g butter
500g cream cheese (I use a mixture of mascarpone and quark, but any soft cream cheese will do)
200g caster sugar
3 eggs
150ml double cream
2 tbsp maple syrup

FOR THE PLUM AND MAPLE SYRUP COMPOTE
8 large ripe plums
3–4 tbsp maple syrup

Place the ginger biscuits in a plastic bag and bash to crumbs using a rolling pin. (You can also do this in a food processor, if you have one.)

Melt the butter gently in a pan and then mix with the biscuit crumbs until you have something that resembles wet sand. Press into the base of a 23cm loose-bottomed cake tin and chill in the fridge for about 15 minutes, while you prepare the filling.

Preheat the oven to 150°C/130°C fan/Gas 2.

Put the cream cheese in a large bowl and mix with a wooden spoon until softened, then add the caster sugar and stir until combined. Add the eggs, one at a time, beating well after each one. Finally add the cream and maple syrup and mix well. Spoon the mixture on top of your biscuit base and bake in the oven for 45 minutes–1 hour. The centre should be just set, but still with a slight wobble. Turn off the oven and leave the cheesecake inside for a further 15 minutes to settle. Remove from the oven and leave to cool before chilling in the fridge for at least 4 hours.

Meanwhile make your 'Plum Divine' (otherwise known as plum and maple syrup compote). Halve, de-stone and quarter the plums and add to a pan with the maple syrup. Place over a low-medium heat and cook for about 8–10 minutes, stirring and squishing the plums, until you have something that looks 'compotey'. Cool and then chill until needed.

To serve, remove the cheesecake from the tin and spoon the plum compote over the top. Cue for a song.

Rock CAKES

-oz S.R. Flour
oz Marg
oz Sugar
.C ½ s
oz Mixed fruit

Ginger bread

Ground Ginger
mixed Spice

treacle
with 1 teaspoon
spices, melt
an stir in
of the beaten
pour into
derate oven about

Put Fruit L
tin 20 minutes

Lyric Theatre   St. Stephen's Day
                                        1973

Dear Miss Sophia T — Thank you for
your letter and for those round things
made of chocolate, rum, sugar, cream
and everything that is BAD for ME.
I gave two to my dog Dorcas, who
asked for a lot more, three others to
friends as a special Christmas treat
and gobbled all the rest myself,
greedily, guzzily, and with huge
enjoyment. They were VERY WELL
MADE of quite WICKED THINGS
Now I am a chocolate balloon.
    Yours cordially, Alec Guinness
                                        P.T.

Cakes, Biscuits & Bites

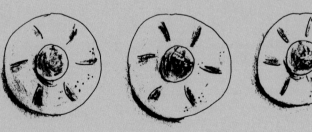

I LOVE lemons. It's official. The shape, the colour, the smell.
Sometimes I buy them because I just want to look at them. I love painting
pictures of lemons, too. When the world gives you lemons, make this cake.
(Did I mention that I LOVE lemons?)

Very Lemony
Almond & Polenta Cake

Prepare in 20 mins · Cook in 45 mins · Serves 8–10

150g polenta
150g ground almonds
150g caster sugar
1 tsp baking powder
200g soft butter, plus extra for greasing
3 large eggs
zest and juice of 3 large lemons
100g icing sugar, sifted
20g flaked almonds, toasted

Preheat the oven to 180°C/160°C fan/Gas 4. Lightly grease and base line a 20cm springform cake tin.

Place the polenta, ground almonds, caster sugar, baking powder and butter in the bowl of a food processor. Blitz together for about 30 seconds to combine. Add the eggs, one at a time, whizzing after each one to incorporate well. Add the lemon zest and whizz again for about 20 seconds. (If you don't have a food processor you can, of course, do all this by hand using a large mixing bowl and spoon.)

Spoon the mixture into your prepared tin and smooth the top. Bake in the centre of the oven for 45 minutes, or until golden and coming away slightly from the edges of the tin.

Meanwhile mix the icing sugar with the lemon juice (about 100ml) in a bowl and whisk together until smooth. When the cake comes out of the oven, use a skewer to make holes all over the top of the cake and, while still warm, pour your lemony syrup over the top.

Scatter over the toasted flaked almonds, while the cake is still sticky, and leave to cool in the tin.

Remove from the tin when cold and serve – splendid on its own or with a big dollop of Whim Wham (see page 158) on the side.

This is an absolute family favourite... and very popular with work colleagues, I've found. It definitely helps to keep it sweet in a rehearsal room. Dancers seem particularly partial to this one in my experience – James would have been ever so pleased.

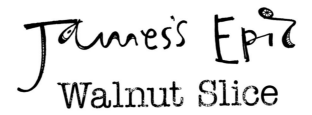

James's Epic
Walnut Slice

Prepare in 30 mins · Cook in 35 mins · Serves 12–16

FOR THE BASE
225g self-raising flour
100g soft butter
50g margarine
100g caster sugar
1 large egg yolk

FOR THE TOPPING
150g apricot jam
4 large egg whites
300g caster sugar
100g walnuts, roughly chopped

Preheat the oven to 180°C/160°C fan/Gas 4. Grease a 20cm square baking tin and line with baking paper.

First make the base. Sift the flour into a large bowl and add the butter and margarine. (My Granny Annie and Uncle James were keen on Stork for baking.) Mix with a wooden spoon, then stir in the caster sugar and egg yolk. Mix really well, bring together with your hands and then press into the prepared tin. Prick all over with a fork and bake in the oven for about 25 minutes, until golden. Leave to cool completely in the tin.

Meanwhile, place the apricot jam in a small pan and heat gently (this will make it easier to spread). Pour over the base and spread evenly in a thin layer.

Put the egg whites, caster sugar and walnuts into a pan and heat gently over a medium heat, stirring continuously. Cook the mixture for about 6–8 minutes, stirring so that it does not stick and burn – many a time I've had to start again! Pour the hot bubbly nutty goo over your apricotty pastry and leave to cool completely in the tin, about 1 hour.

Remove from the tin and cut into squares. Share with those who understand.

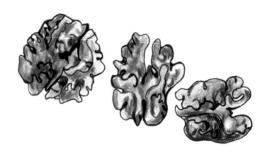

My mum-in-law, Anne, is a FAB cook, but she doesn't think she is. When she reads this she will shriek, hold her head in embarrassment and deny it all vociferously. I took the liberty of adding the figs.

Anne's
Irish Brack Bread

Prepare in 20 mins, plus soaking overnight · Cook in 1¼ hours · Makes 8–10 slices

**250g mixture of raisins, currants
  and sultanas**
**200g mixture of dates, prunes and apricots,
  de-stoned and chopped**
150g soft brown sugar
2 tea bags
2 large eggs, lightly beaten
300g self-raising flour
½ tsp salt
4 fresh figs, trimmed and thinly sliced

The evening before, put all the dried fruits and brown sugar in a bowl. Brew the tea bags in 350ml boiling water for 5 minutes. Pour the tea over the dried fruits, give everything a stir and leave to soak overnight at room temperature.

Preheat the oven to 180°C/160°C fan/Gas 4 and grease and line a 1kg loaf tin.

Add the eggs to the tea-soaked fruits and mix well, then sift in the flour and salt and stir until well combined. Pour half the mixture into your prepared tin and add about half the sliced figs in a layer. Cover with the remaining cake mixture and top with the remaining figs.

Bake in the oven for 1¼ hours, covering with foil after 45 minutes. Leave to cool in the tin for 10–15 minutes, before turning out on to a wire rack.

Gorgeous with cheese.
Or lots of butter and jam.
Or just lots of butter.
Or just on its own.

This recipe arose because of our apple tree and its generosity. This is a really comforting cakey cake. Nothing fairy or cup going on here. It's a robust individual that would fight its way out of a paper case in disgust, singing a song about not having its style cramped. It's a little bit audacious, tempted?

Toffee Apple Cake

Prepare in 30 mins · Cook in 1¼ hours · Serves 8–10

FOR THE CAKE
175g soft butter, plus extra for greasing
150g granulated sugar
4 large eggs, lightly beaten
200g self-raising flour
1 tsp vanilla extract
150g ground almonds
1 tsp baking powder
3 large eating apples (about 400g), peeled, cored and thinly sliced

FOR THE TOFFEE SAUCE
100g butter
100g light muscovado sugar
150ml double cream

Preheat the oven to 160°C/140°C fan/Gas 3. Grease and base line two 20cm loose-bottomed cake tins.

First make your toffee sauce by melting all the ingredients together in a pan over a low heat and stirring and bubbling until golden, about 2 minutes. Set aside to cool.

Put the butter and sugar in the bowl of an electric mixer and cream together until pale. Gradually add the beaten eggs, adding a large spoonful of flour after each to stop the mixture curdling. Once the eggs are combined, beat in the vanilla extract, then add the remaining flour, ground almonds and baking powder. Fold in well.

Pour half the mixture into your prepared tin and spread in an even layer. Arrange half the apple slices in a swirled layer, then spoon over half the toffee sauce. Repeat with the remaining cake mixture, apples and toffee sauce (leave a bit of toffee sauce for final drizzling, if you can). Bake in the oven for 1 hour–1 hour 10 minutes (check for doneness with a skewer after 1 hour). The cake will rise up during baking and can drip goo over the edge, so place a foil-lined tray underneath to catch any toffee drips.

Remove from the oven and leave to cool in the tin for at least 45 minutes before unmoulding. Drizzle with the remaining toffee sauce and serve warm with ice cream or cold with hot tea.

I used to be mesmerised as a child in the back kitchen of Uncle James's tearooms, as invariably there was a huge paddle mixer going round and round and round with orange cake mix or chocolate cake mix, smooth and shiny with a wonderful consistency slooping on the sides of the big silver bowl. I think this cake is worth it just for the smell alone.

James's 100g Orange Cake

Prepare in 30 mins · Cook in 20 mins · Serves 8–10

FOR THE SPONGE
100g margarine (I like Stork)
100g soft butter
100g caster sugar
100g demerara sugar
finely grated zest and juice of 1 orange
4 large eggs, lightly beaten
200g self-raising flour
1 heaped tsp baking powder

FOR THE FILLING
250ml freshly squeezed orange juice
finely grated zest of 1 orange
25g cornflour
2 large egg yolks
50g caster sugar
20g soft butter

FOR THE ICING
100g soft butter
200g icing sugar, sifted
finely grated zest of 1 orange
1–2 tbsp orange juice

Terry's Chocolate Orange, broken in
    segments, to decorate

Preheat the oven to 180°C/160°C fan/Gas 4 and lightly grease two 18cm cake tins and line the bases with baking paper. My Granny Annie, who was a cook and maid in the olden days, always kept butter wrappers in the fridge for such a task and I still do that to this day.

Cream together the margarine, butter, sugars and orange zest, either in a stand mixer or in a large bowl with some electric beaters, until pale and fluffy. Add the eggs one at a time, beating well after each one (add a spoonful of flour if the mixture looks like it's curdling). Sift in the flour and baking powder and fold well to combine, then stir in the orange juice.

Divide the cake mixture between the cake tins and bake on the middle shelf of the oven for 20 minutes, or until golden and springy to the touch. Leave to cool in the tin for a few minutes before turning out on to a wire rack.

Meanwhile make your orange filling. Put the orange juice and zest in a pan and sift in the cornflour. Heat gently, stirring all the time. After a few minutes it will come to a simmer and start to thicken, so keep an eye on it – the last time I did this I walked away for a mo and it all went a bit lumpy! Remove from the heat and add the egg yolks, caster sugar and butter. Transfer to a bowl and leave to cool. When the cakes are cool, sandwich them together with the orange custard filling.

Make an orange butter icing by beating together the soft butter, icing sugar and orange zest. Gradually add the orange juice until it's a good consistency and spread over the top of the cake. Finally decorate with segments of Terry's chocolate orange. There will be some segments left... for the cook, of course.

Our eldest, Ernie, is my brownie judge. I don't want to sound like a smug mug, but he did give these high marks because they are so simple. He is not one for the fancy brownie. I have brought home all manner of fancy-pants ones from wonderful places where I couldn't resist, and often they have got no more than a raised eyebrow and a deep sigh... 'Too fancy, Mum'. Sometimes it pays to keep things simple.

Three Choc Button
Brownies

Prepare in 15 mins · Cook in 15–18 mins · Makes 12–14

100g milk chocolate
100g dark chocolate
100g gluten-free self-raising flour
100g soft brown sugar
100g ground almonds
3 large eggs
1 tsp vanilla extract
100g white chocolate, chopped
white chocolate buttons or Smarties
**   (optional), to decorate**

Preheat the oven to 180°C/160°C fan/Gas 4. Grease a 20cm square tin and line with baking paper.

Melt the milk and dark chocolate in a bain-marie: break the chocolate into pieces, put in a heatproof bowl and set over a pan of just-simmering water, making sure the base of the bowl doesn't touch the water.

Once melted, stir into the flour, sugar, ground almonds, eggs and vanilla and mix well. Gently fold in the chopped white chocolate and spoon into your prepared tin. Bake in the oven for 15–18 minutes, until just coming away from the sides of the tin but still pleasingly squidgy in the centre.

Leave to cool in the tin before cutting into fingers and decorating with white chocolate buttons. We have been known to use Smarties to make traffic-light brownies – simple pleasures.

Sometimes all the bananas get eaten, sometimes they don't and a wee mottled bunch sits sadly on the side gathering frenzied fruit flies... banana bread to the rescue!

Banana Bread

Prepare in 10 mins · Cook in 1 hour · Serves 8–10

100g soft butter
100g caster sugar
2 large eggs
200g self-raising flour
1 tsp vanilla extract
1 tsp baking powder
1 tsp bicarbonate of soda
4–5 ripe bananas (about 400g peeled),
   mashed

FOR THE TOPPING
150g caster sugar
2 tbsp water
150 double cream
dried banana chips, to decorate

Preheat the oven to 180°C/160°C fan/Gas 4 and line a 1kg loaf tin with baking paper.

In the bowl of an electric mixer with a paddle attachment, put the butter, sugar, eggs, flour and vanilla extract. Alternatively use a large bowl and a handheld electric mixer. Beat on medium speed for a few minutes, until everything is well combined. Stir in the baking powder and bicarbonate of soda and mashed bananas. Turn into the prepared tin and smooth the surface with the back of a spoon. Loosely cover the tin with baking paper or foil and bake in the middle of the oven for 45 minutes– 1 hour, removing the paper or foil for the last 20 minutes.

Meanwhile make the toffee topping. Melt the caster sugar and water in a pan and then bubble over a medium heat until golden. Reduce the heat and then beat in the double cream (take care as the mixture will splutter). Mix until smooth and then transfer to a bowl to cool.

When the cake is ready, leave to settle in the tin for 10 minutes before turning out on to a wire rack. When it is still just warm, transfer to a plate. Spread with the toffee topping and decorate with dried banana chips, or whatever tickles your fancy.

I'm very partial to an all-in-one sort of cake and this is, I think, a very festive one. I made it as a celebration cake for my mum when she was awarded an OBE (for goodness' sake), for her services to the arts and charity. I should really rename it the 'Proud Daughter Cake'. But if I did Mum might well kill me, be stripped of her honour forthwith and clapped in the Tower. Then I would just have to make a special version with a file secreted inside.

Honey Hazelnut Cake

Prepare in 30 mins · Cook in 20–25 mins · Serves 8–10

FOR THE CAKE
125g roasted hazelnuts
6 large egg yolks
200g runny honey
125g plain flour
50g soft butter

400g mascarpone
3–4 heaped tbsp icing sugar, sifted
1 tsp vanilla extract
300g raspberries
50g flaked almonds, toasted

Preheat the oven to 180°C/160°C fan/Gas 4 and grease and line the bases of two 20cm loose-bottomed cake tins. Blitz the hazelnuts in a food processor until they are as fine as possible and set aside.

Mix the egg yolks and honey together in a large mixing bowl until well combined. Add the ground hazelnuts, flour and butter and mix until blended. Divide equally between the two cake tins and level out the tops.

Bake in the oven for 20–25 minutes until good and golden. Leave to cool in the tins for about 10 minutes, then turn out on to a wire rack to cool completely. Be not alarmed – this is not a rising sponge but you will achieve height with your raspberry and mascarpone layers.

Meanwhile, tip the mascarpone into a mixing bowl and soften with a wooden spoon. Add the icing sugar, to taste, and vanilla extract. Spread about half of this lovely, vanillary mascarpone over one of the cakes and then arrange half the raspberries over the top. Place the other sponge on top, spread with the remaining mascarpone and decorate with the remaining raspberries and the flaked almonds. Chill until needed, removing about 30 minutes before serving.

I also do a gluten-free version of this with gluten-free flour... for those gluten-free-ers.

This is from an old gingerbread recipe of my Granny Annie's that I'd written out as a child. I've jazzed it up a bit, I confess. Granny Annie was in service as a cook and she would never have dreamt of including alcohol in a recipe. She was quite religious and had *The Light of the World* on her bedroom wall. She made rock cakes every Friday, and always made a special batch without peel for me because I didn't like it. I remember the little me really appreciating that. This is a very gingery whisky loaf, and even with a spot of the old Scottish brew in it I hope Granny Annie would give it a thumbs up.

Granny Annie's
Ginger and Whisky Loaf

Prepare in 20 mins · Cook in 1¼ hours · Serves 8–10

FOR THE CAKE
150ml whole milk
75g golden syrup
75g black treacle
4 pieces of stem ginger, drained and finely chopped, plus 4 tsp of syrup from the jar
125g soft butter, plus extra for greasing
300g plain flour
4 tsp ground ginger
1 tsp mixed spice
150g soft brown sugar
1 heaped tsp bicarbonate of soda
3 tbsp whisky

FOR THE WHISKY ICING
225g icing sugar, sifted
100g soft butter
1 tsp vanilla extract
2 tbsp whisky
2 pieces of stem ginger, drained and chopped, to decorate

Put the milk, syrup, treacle, chopped ginger and ginger syrup in a pan and place over a low heat, stirring until combined. Remove from the heat and leave to cool to room temperature. Meanwhile preheat the oven to 160°C140°C fan/Gas 3 and grease a 1kg loaf tin and line with baking paper.

Put the butter and flour in a large bowl and rub together until the mixture resembles fine breadcrumbs. Add the ground ginger, mixed spice and brown sugar and stir well. Add the cooled gingery, syrupy milk and use a large whisk or spatula to combine until smooth. Fold in the bicarbonate of soda and then spoon into your prepared tin. Bake in the oven for 1–1¼ hours.

To make a whisky icing, put the icing sugar, butter, vanilla and whisky in a bowl and whisk together until smooth. Chill in the fridge until needed.

Test to see if the cake is done by inserting a skewer into the centre; it should come out cleanish (I like mine not too done). Pierce the cake all over with the skewer and then drizzle over the whisky. Leave to cool in the tin before turning out on to a wire rack. When completely cool, top with the icing and decorate with pieces of stem ginger.

OCH AYE!

I have a particular fondness for the Bakewell Tart. Richard and I were married in Birchover, Derbyshire and had a big pile of Bakewell tarts instead of a wedding cake. We decided that wedding cake often got left in boxes and missed out on all the fun, so we chose the indigenous no-frills Bakewell. I seem to remember they came up trumps.

Bakewell Tart

Prepare in 15 mins, plus resting · Cook in 1 hour · Serves 8–10

320g ready-rolled shortcrust pastry sheet
200g soft butter
200g caster sugar
3 large eggs, beaten
½ tsp almond extract
200g ground almonds
6 tbsp raspberry jam
1–2 tbsp flaked almonds, lightly toasted
icing sugar, to decorate

Take the pastry out of the fridge about 15 minutes before using, to allow it to soften slightly. Preheat the oven to 180°C/160°C fan/Gas 4.

Unwrap the pastry and roll it out to a circle big enough to line a loose-bottomed fluted tart tin, about 22cm in diameter. Carefully press the pastry into the edges and let any excess pastry hang over the edges for now. Line with baking paper and fill with baking beans and then blind bake for about 15 minutes. Remove the beans and paper and cook for a further 5 minutes to crisp up the base.

In a large bowl, mix together the butter, sugar, beaten eggs, almond extract and ground almonds until well combined. Spread the jam evenly over the pastry base and then spoon the almond mixture over the top. Trim the overhanging pastry so there is about 3cm all round and then fold this excess pastry over the filling.

Place on a baking tray and bake in the middle of your oven for about 40 minutes. Allow to cool completely in the tin before removing. Scatter with the lightly toasted flaked almonds, dust with icing sugar and serve.

Put the kettle on someone.

These were my favourite things to make in my Uncle James's tearoom. You would sit at the kitchen table with all the prepared ingredients and assemble them like edible puzzles. Wee hillocks of pineappley creamy custardy wonderful memories.

Uncle James's Pineapple Tarts

Prepare in 45 mins, plus chilling · Cook in 30 mins · Serves 8

FOR THE SWEET PASTRY
225g plain flour, plus extra for dusting
110g soft butter
80g caster sugar
1 large egg

FOR THE CUSTARD FILLING
500ml whole milk
120g caster sugar
4 large egg yolks
25g cornflour, sifted
25g plain flour, sifted

FOR THE TOPPING
225ml double cream
200g icing sugar, sifted
1 generous slice of fresh pineapple
drop of yellow food colouring

First make the pastry. Place the flour and butter in a large bowl and rub together until the mixture resembles breadcrumbs. Stir in the sugar and add the egg. Mix with your hands until it starts to come together and gather into a dough. Wrap in cling film and chill in the fridge for 30 minutes.

Next make your custard. Pour the milk into a pan and heat until just scalding. Meanwhile put the sugar and egg yolks in a bowl and whisk until pale, then fold in the cornflour and flour. Gradually pour about half the hot milk into the bowl and whisk continuously to combine. Pour the whole lot back into the pan with the remaining milk and keep whisking over a medium heat until it thickens. Transfer to a bowl and leave to cool to room temperature. (A sheet of cling film placed on the surface of the custard will prevent a skin forming.) Chill in the fridge.

Preheat the oven to 180°C/160°C fan/Gas 4. Roll out the pastry on a floured surface and then use to line a jam tart tin (a 9cm cutter should do the trick). Then line each tin with baking paper, fill with baking beans and bake in the oven for 10–12 minutes. Remove the paper and beans and cook for a further 5 minutes to crisp up the bases. Remove from the oven and when cool enough to handle, turn out and cool on wire rack.

Meanwhile, whip the cream until soft peaks form; chill. Sift the icing sugar into a bowl. Squeeze the juice from your pineapple slice into another bowl – chop the squeezed pineapple into small pieces and set aside (this goes into the tart and on top). Stir the juice gradually into the icing sugar until you get a drizzle consistency – add a tiny drop of yellow food colouring.

Now for the assembly – hooray! Take a cooled sweet pastry case and put a teaspoon of custard into the bottom. Add a teaspoon of chopped pineapple, cover with a hillock of whipped cream (I do this with a little butter knife). Finish with a drizzle of pineapple icing and garnish with some lovely pineapple pieces.

JOY! These will need eating within a few hours of assembly (as if you need telling).

These are our family version of flapjacks. Because we always make them in Scotland we call them flap jocks. Our son Walter and his mate Archie renamed them 'Flappy Jocks'... let's not go there.
They are the simplest of flappy jocks ever.

Flap Jocks

Prepare in 5 mins · Cook in 10 mins · Makes about 15

250g butter (I know, hardcore)
450g golden syrup (or 1 small tin)
350–400g porridge oats

Preheat the oven to 180°C/160°C fan/Gas 4. Lightly grease and line a shallow 25 x 20cm baking tray.

Put the butter and syrup in a heavy-based pan and place over a medium heat. Stir until the butter has melted, then bubble away for about 5–8 minutes, stirring occasionally, until the mixture is a rich golden colour. You are looking for it to reach soft ball consistency (see page 195).

Remove from the heat and stir in the oats. You don't want the mixture to become too dry and stodgy, so you may not need all the oats. Add them slowly and stir well between each addition.

Tip the mixture into your prepared tin and bake on the middle shelf of the oven for about 10 minutes. Keep an eye out for any overbrowning at the edges; flap jocks have to be chewy and too long in the oven will kill the chew. Remove and leave to cool in the tin. After about 5 minutes, score into squares or rectangles with a knife and leave to cool fully in the tin before turning out.

This is buttery, chewy stuff. If there's a damp, heathery hill to walk up during the chew all the better. Very fine on the Northern line, too.

These buns are inspired by my very first and favourite recipe book, which I still have: *My Fun to Cook Book*. I used it with the boys when they were little, too. The book is practically in pieces, and smeared with ancient chocolate, egg, etc. A bit like me after a day in the kitchen.

Prepare in 25 mins · Cook in 30 mins · Makes 12

FOR THE BUTTERSCOTCH SAUCE
200ml double cream
150g butter
150g soft light brown sugar

FOR THE SPONGE
50g margarine
50g soft butter
200g caster sugar
1 tsp vanilla extract
3 large eggs
200g self-raising flour
1 tsp baking powder
50g glacé cherries, chopped
30g flaked almonds

First make the butterscotch sauce. Put the cream, butter and sugar in a small pan and melt gently, then bubble over a low heat until a light golden colour, about 5 minutes. Pour into a large bowl and leave to cool completely, stirring occasionally.

Preheat the oven to 180°C/160°C fan/Gas 4 and grease a 12-hole cupcake tin with butter.

Now for the sponge. Cream together the margarine, butter and caster sugar, either in a stand mixer or in a large bowl with

electric beaters. Add the vanilla extract and the eggs one by one, beating well after each addition. Sift in the flour and baking powder and fold until all combined.

Divide the chopped cherries and flaked almonds between the holes in the tin and then add a spoonful of butterscotch sauce to each one. Top with the cake mixture and bake on the middle shelf of the oven for 15–20 minutes, or until golden.

Leave to cool in the tin for 5 minutes before carefully lifting each one out and turning upside down. Don't worry if you have to spoon the cherries and almonds out of the tin and squish them back on to the cake – we're going for the rustic look. Squiggle with a little more of your butterscotch sauce. You'll almost certainly have some butterscotch sauce left over but this isn't usually a problem – I just pop it in a jar and use it on ice cream or poached pears or a spoon...

Hallelujah!

I know – 'salted', 'caramel', 'drizzle', 'choc' – have I over-egged the cookie? I remember receiving a Brownie Badge for making biscuits. When I first made these I must admit the boys' 'Oohs' and 'Ahhhhs' felt ten times better than that proudly received Brownie badge. (I was a Pixie – in them days you could garner a badge from learning to fold a man's shirt properly – I kid you not.)

Salted Caramel Cookies &
White Chocolate Drizzle

Prepare in 15 mins · Cook in 7–8 mins · Makes 12

FOR THE SALTED CARAMEL
100g butter
100g soft brown sugar
¼–½ tsp sea salt flakes, to taste
100ml double cream

FOR THE DOUGH
100g butter
100g caster sugar
100g soft brown sugar
2 tbsp vegetable oil
1 large egg
1 tsp vanilla extract
200g plain flour
pinch of salt
1 tsp baking powder

150g white chocolate, broken into pieces

Preheat the oven to 200°C/180°C fan/Gas 6 and line a baking tray with baking paper.

First make the salted caramel by melting the butter and the sugar together in a heavy-based pan over a low heat until it's all bubbly and almost creamy, stirring gently. This should take about 5–8 minutes. Remove from the heat and slowly stir in the salt and the cream. Set aside.

Now for the dough. Cream the butter and sugars together in a large bowl until well combined. Stir in the oil, egg and vanilla and mix well. Gradually sift in the flour, salt and baking powder and mix together until you have a soft dough.

Roll spoonfuls of dough into balls and place on your prepared tray – a good distance apart. Don't be tempted to flatten them too much. I always end up doing two batches or using two trays. Dip your finger in some flour and use to make a wee puddle hole in the middle of each blob; fill with your salted caramel. Bake in the oven for about 7–8 minutes, or until just golden.

Remove from the oven and slather each hot bubbly biscuit with another teaspoon of salted caramel. Cool on a wire rack.

While the biscuits are cooling, melt the white chocolate in a bain-marie. Place in a small heatproof bowl set over a pan of just-simmering water, making sure the bottom of the bowl doesn't touch the water. Take care not to overheat, as white chocolate burns easily. Remove from the heat and drizzle over your caramel cookies.

Burst into song! Share with the group!

A couple of years ago I joined a brilliant endeavour called the Casserole Club. It's an initiative for sharing food in your neighbourhood. It might be for someone who can't get out much, or an elderly neighbour or someone on their own who could do with a spot of sustenance – essentially it's connecting up via food. Edith is from Switzerland, though she's lived over here since the 1940s. She is 95, and such a laugh. We've made friends via the Casserole Club, and these delicious traditional Swiss biscuits are from her.

Edith's Leckerli

Prepare in 15 mins · Cook in 25 mins · Makes 15

200g runny honey
100g caster sugar
170g ground almonds
100g chopped mixed peel
2 tsp ground cinnamon
1 tsp ground cloves
6 tbsp kirsch
290g plain flour
finely grated zest of 1 orange
finely grated zest of 1 lemon

FOR THE TOPPING
100g caster sugar
sugar strands or stars, to decorate

Preheat the oven to 180°C/160°C fan/Gas 4. Lightly grease a 30 x 20cm baking tin and line with baking paper.

Melt the honey and sugar together in a large pan over a medium heat, stirring well. Remove from the heat and stir in the ground almonds, mixed peel, cinnamon, cloves and kirsch.

Stir in the flour and the orange and lemon zest. It should form a pleasingly sticky dough. Spoon into the prepared tin and, using damp hands, press into the edges of the tin until even. (Don't worry if it doesn't quite reach the edges.)

Bake in the oven for 20 minutes, until set. Leave to cool in the tray for 5 minutes before cutting into squares. Edith says leckerli should always be square.

Prepare the topping by putting the caster sugar in a pan with 2 tablespoons of water and placing over a medium heat until melted. Increase the heat until the caramel starts bubbling and turning pale gold, about 5 minutes. Brush over the top of your leckerli and then sprinkle with sugar strands or stars. Leave to cool completely in the tin. These can be stored in an airtight container for up to 10 days.

Ding Dong Merrily on High!

Mum always made these with the meringues at Christmas... but I do remember her crying once making brandy snaps – they kept breaking and it was one of those overtired-at-Christmas moments that put me off making them for years. She wrote in her book, 'Sophie caught me sobbing and whimpering one Christmas when my brandy snaps didn't work. She has hated them ever since.'

There was a *MasterChef* task involving brandy snaps and it brought it all back – but in a way that made me want to reclaim them for Mum from that tearful episode all those years ago. They really are quite fun. Honest.

Mum's Brandy Snaps

Prepare in 15 mins · Cook in 6–8 mins · Makes about 16

100g butter
100g caster sugar
100g golden syrup
100g plain flour
1 tsp ground ginger
juice of ½ lemon

Preheat the oven to 180°C/160°C fan/Gas 4 and line a couple of baking trays with baking paper.

Put the butter, sugar and golden syrup into a heavy-based pan and heat gently over a low-medium heat until the sugar has dissolved. Remove from the heat and then add the flour, ground ginger and lemon juice. Stir together until you have a beautiful liquidy ginger biscuit mixture.

Drop teaspoons of the mixture on to your prepared trays – you need to work quickly once these are baked, so it's best to work in batches – you should be able to fit 4–6 on one tray. Bake in the oven for 6–8 minutes, but the cooking time will vary so keep an eye on them. When the mixture is a nice golden colour, take out and let rest for just a moment or two.

I use a small thin cucumber (yes, really!) for this bit but my mum uses a lightly oiled wooden spoon handle so you might find this or even a thin rolling pin works for you. Gently roll each snap off the paper around your cucumber/wooden spoon and press gently to close. Slide on to a wire rack to firm up completely while you roll the rest. Repeat the baking and rolling until all your mixture is used up.

My boys like these empty as they are not mad about creamy stuff, but you can fill as you wish with either some whipped cream mixed with a little icing sugar and some ground ginger, or whipped cream mixed with a splash of brandy. The brandy snap is your oyster...

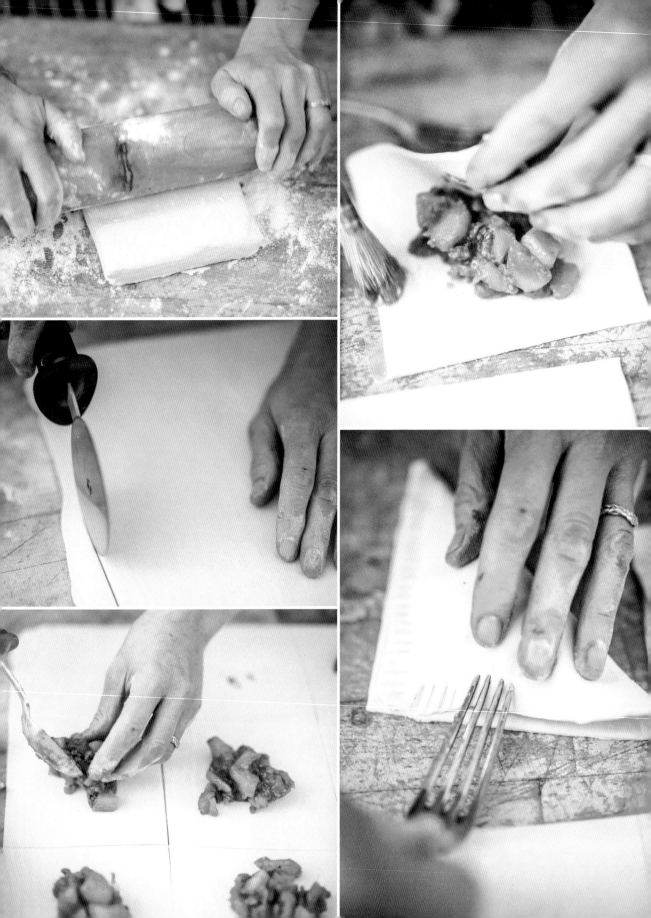

These came about because of our apple tree: it's a very giving tree! They're a great quick treat on a rainy day after school... especially if your children have a couple of friends over. They don't keep brilliantly so are best eaten fresh, although there never seems to be a problem with that in our house. (There are three growing boys living next door, too, who are extremely appreciative.)

Apple & Pecan Turnovers

Prepare in 30 mins · Cook in 40 mins · Makes 9

100g butter, plus extra for brushing
100g soft brown sugar
800g eating apples, peeled, cored and chopped into 2cm pieces
1 generous tsp ground cinnamon
1 tbsp cornflour
30g pecan nuts, chopped
500g ready-made puff pastry (take out of the fridge 10 minutes before rolling)
1 egg, beaten, to glaze
50g granulated sugar

Melt the butter and brown sugar together in a large non-stick frying pan over a medium heat. Add the apple pieces and cinnamon (add a bit more if you are cinnamon mad!) and let the mixture bubble for about 10 minutes over a low heat, until the apples have softened.

Put the cornflour in a small bowl and add a couple of tablespoons of hot liquid from the pan to it. Mix until smooth and then pour back into the bubbling apple mix. Stir and let the mixture quietly thicken over a low heat for 2 minutes. Mix in the chopped pecans and tip the whole lot into a large

bowl and leave to cool for about 15–20 minutes. Meanwhile preheat the oven to 200°C/180°C fan/Gas 6.

Roll out the pastry on a lightly floured surface into a large rectangle. Use a sharp knife to neaten the edges and then divide and cut the pastry into 9 squares.

Divide the apple mixture between the pastry squares, placing just off centre. Brush the edges of the pastry with beaten egg and then fold one corner over the filling to make a triangle and press to seal, using a fork to mark the pastry. Transfer to a large baking tray.

Mix the granulated sugar with a tablespoon of hot water in a pan and heat until melted. Brush the syrup over your turnovers and bake in the oven for about 25 minutes.

Remove from the oven and leave for about 10 minutes before serving – the filling will be hot! These are best served warm and are definitely best on the day they are made.

My mum always made a big batch of meringues at Christmas. She stored them in a huge glass jar. I got very adept at pinching a meringue in the night and rearranging the jar so it didn't look like any had gone. Sneaky. Not that I want to drag any of you down to my level of petty crime... but I warn you there is a risk.

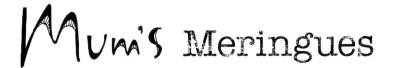

Mum's Meringues

Prepare in 15 mins · Cook in 1½–2 hours · Makes about 14

6 egg whites
340g caster sugar

Preheat the oven to 120°C/100°C fan/Gas ½ and line two baking trays with baking paper. My mum used to dust her baking trays very lightly with flour to stop the meringues sticking, so that's what I do, but you may find that non-stick baking paper does the job.

Put your egg whites in a large, clean bowl and whisk them on medium speed with an electric whisk, until stiff peaks form. Increase the speed to medium-high and start adding the caster sugar, a tablespoon at a time, whisking well after each addition. Your mixture will start to look thick, glossy, silky and eminently lickable.

Scoop up tablespoons of the mixture and use a dessert spoon to ease it on to your baking trays. Bake on the lower shelves of your oven for 1½–2 hours, swapping the trays around halfway through the cooking time. Check them after 1½ hours – the meringues should be pale golden and sound 'crisp' when tapped gently. With meringues it's really more about drying out than cooking, so when you think they are done turn off the oven, leave the door open and let them cool inside.

This is a great recipe to do when you are doing other stuff in the kitchen too, so you can keep an eye on them and do your checking and swapping.

This is dedicated to my utterly awesome niece, Gaia.

We have a home in Scotland still, and you have to love rain to love Scotland. It's handy if you love tablet too, because Scottish tablet almost makes up for the rain – and the midges... almost.

Rainy Day Tablet

Prepare in 10 mins · Cook in 20 mins · Makes about 40 pieces

500g granulated sugar
50g butter, plus extra for greasing
250ml whole milk
1 tbsp golden syrup
1 tsp vanilla extract

Lightly grease a shallow baking tin. A good size for this recipe is about 25 x 18cm but you could easily use a bigger tin and just double up the quantities – the more the merrier!

Put the sugar, butter, milk and syrup in a large, heavy-based pan and bring slowly to the boil, stirring so that the sugar dissolves. Keep boiling, stirring all the while, for about 10 minutes until the mixture turns a lovely golden colour and the temperature reaches 115°C. If you don't have a sugar thermometer, test using the soft ball method: drop a blob of mixture into a small saucer or dish of cold water. Push gently with your finger – it should have the consistency of a soft ball. If it's a runny blob, return to the heat but stay vigilant and keep stirring until you have the right consistency. You want tablet, not the chewy stuff that pulls your fillings out.

Remove from the heat and add the vanilla extract, then beat the mixture for a good 3–5 minutes, until it starts to go grainy or crystallised. Pour quickly into your tin and leave to cool and set for about 30 minutes, then cut into squares. (You can speed this up by chilling in the fridge, if you can't wait.)

These are dedicated to my ridiculously brilliant nephew, Tindy...
don't ask why!

Boobie Cakes

Prepare in 30 mins · Cook in 15 mins · Makes about 20

3 large egg whites
½ tsp cream of tartar
150g caster sugar
150g desiccated coconut
150g coconut flakes
1 tsp vanilla extract

TO DECORATE
100g white chocolate, broken into pieces
10 glacé cherries, halved

Preheat the oven to 180°C/160°C fan/Gas 4 and line two baking trays with baking paper.

In a large bowl, whisk the egg whites with the cream of tartar until soft peaks form. Add the sugar and whisk again until thick, glossy and shiny. Fold in the desiccated coconut, coconut flakes and vanilla and mix until combined.

Use two spoons to pile into mounds on the prepared trays. Shape them into little volcanos with your hands and then bake in the oven for 15–20 minutes, until the top and sides colour and the boobies lift easily off the paper. Transfer to a wire rack to cool.

Melt the white chocolate in a heatproof bowl set over a pan of simmering water (making sure the bottom of the bowl doesn't touch the water). Decorate each cooked Boobie with a blob of melted chocolate and a cherry half.

VARIATION
COCONUT AND CHESTNUT CHEEKIES
(makes about 10)

Follow the recipe above but omit the coconut flakes and increase the amount of desiccated coconut to 300g. Make a filling by whisking 200ml of double cream until thick and then folding in 125g sweetened chestnut purée (crème de marrons). Chill the filling for 1–2 hours before using. When the macaroons are cool, sandwich them together with the chestnut cream. Melt 75g dark chocolate and drizzle over the cheekies to serve.

My dad loved Garibaldi biscuits. He used to call them dead fly cemeteries. My husband Richard was brought up in the Peak District. So was this recipe. I found it at my in-laws' when they still lived there and I loved the mint addition. Garibaldi biscuits originated in Stoke-on-Trent, apparently. They were named after an Italian general and invented by a Scot called John Carr (of Water Biscuit fame.) Thank you heartily, Mr Carr.

Dead Fly Biscuits

Prepare in 10 mins, plus resting · Cook in 20 mins · Makes about 20

320g ready-made shortcrust pastry
50g (very) soft butter
150g currants
50g caster sugar, plus extra for sprinkling
1 heaped tsp mixed spice
8 large mint leaves, finely chopped
1 egg white, beaten

Take the pastry out of the fridge about 10 minutes before using, to allow it to soften slightly. Preheat the oven to 180°C/160°C fan/Gas 4 and line a large baking tray with baking paper.

Unwrap the pastry and gently roll out on a floured surface so that it takes the shape of a long oblong. It should be about 2mm thick.

Use a large knife to spread the butter over one half of the pastry sheet. Mix together the currants, sugar, mixed spice and chopped mint leaves in a bowl and sprinkle evenly over the butter. Then fold one half of the pastry over the other half to cover the filling. Run your rolling pin over the pastry again, until the currants start to show through.

Transfer the pastry to your lined baking tray and then brush the top with beaten egg white. Sprinkle over a couple of tablespoons of caster sugar and bake in the oven for 20 minutes or until golden. Cool on a wire rack, then cut into oblongs – whatever size you fancy!

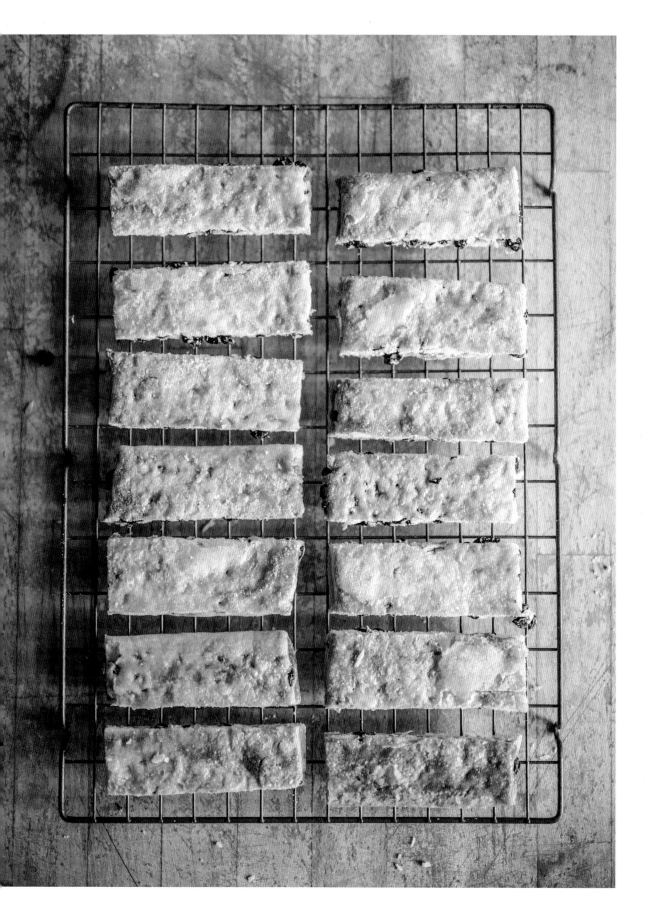

My Granny Megsie really was a natural, wonderful cook. She even attended the West of Scotland College of Domestic Science, affectionately known as 'The Dough School' and now, Glasgow Caledonian University. She used to make little whistley noises around the kitchen as she created, which was very soothing. (It's something I realise *I* do now.) Plus, her old Rayburn was always on as it heated the house and dried our socks and everything, so her kitchen was the cosiest place to be in every sense of the word. My boys love this... What am I saying, we ALL do! It's a real crowd pleaser.

Granny Megsie's
Millionaire Shortbread

Prepare in 40 mins · Cook in 30 mins · Makes 16 squares

FOR THE BASE
100g rice flour
100g polenta
100g semolina
100g caster sugar
125g soft butter, plus extra for greasing
1 large egg

FOR THE TOPPING
175g butter
175g caster sugar
397g can condensed milk
100g dark chocolate, broken into pieces
100g milk chocolate, broken into pieces

Preheat the oven to 170°C/150° fan/Gas 3 and lightly butter a 20 x 20cm Swiss roll tin.

Put all the ingredients for the base into a food processor and pulse to combine. Bring it together into a dough and press into the tin. Prick all over with a fork and bake in the oven for 25 minutes, until pale golden in colour. Leave to cool in the tin.

Meanwhile make the caramel. Melt the butter, sugar and condensed milk in a pan over a low heat, stirring all the time. Let it bubble away for about 5 minutes, stirring so that it doesn't catch on the bottom of the pan. When a light golden colour, pour over the cooled shortbread base. (That pan, when cooled, is THE best for a small person to clean with a spoon and a mouth.)

Megsie always melted one bar of milk and one bar of plain choc, so that's what I do too. Break the chocolate into pieces and put in a heatproof bowl set over a pan of just-simmering water (make sure the bottom of the bowl doesn't touch the water). Pour the melted chocolate over the caramel layer and chill in the fridge – away from prying eyes – until set. If you remember, score it into portions with a knife before it is fully set to make cutting easier. Best served at room temperature.

Note: You can replace the polenta and semolina with 200g of plain flour if you like. It's just as good, just a bit less crumbly.

We all have our favourite 'Top Snack', and this is Ernie's. My mum used to make a version of this for anyone feeling a bit blue or over-tired. She would squash lots of soft brown sugar and cinnamon on to a slice of bread and toast it until it went bubbly. The smell and the comfort of it! Three or four ingredients and you've got a metaphorical fireside on toast.

Ern's
Cinnamon Toast

Prepare in 5 mins · Cook in 5–6 mins · Serves 1

2 eggs
1 tbsp demerara or granulated sugar
2 tsp ground cinnamon
2 slices of bread
butter and oil, for frying
maple syrup and sliced banana (optional),
   to serve

Beat the eggs together with the sugar and cinnamon and pour into a shallow bowl (one that is big enough to hold two slices of bread). Soak your bread slices in the lovely sweet cinnamon goo, turning so that both sides are coated.

Heat a small knob of butter and a splash of oil in a non-stick frying pan over a medium heat. Add the eggy cinnamon bread and fry for about 3 minutes on each side, or until golden.

Serve your eggy cinnamon toast with maple syrup and sliced banana if you're partial. If you are anything like Ern, you will be enjoying this quite late at night.

The boys love these griddles in the morning with maple syrup and blueberries or bananas or Nutella. They would be lovely with bacon and eggs, too. They are a cross between a pancake and a crumpet, I think. A friend at college used to serve them up with homemade hot chocolate of heart-stopping richness.

Prepare in 5 mins · Cook in 8 mins · Makes about 10–12

50g butter, plus extra for greasing
100g caster sugar
250ml milk
2 eggs, beaten
200g self-raising flour
½ tsp salt
2 tsp baking powder

Preheat the oven to 200°C/180°C fan/Gas 6.

Melt the butter in a small pan and tip into a large cool bowl. Add the caster sugar and stir to combine, then mix in the milk and then the eggs. Sift in the flour and whisk to make sure you don't end up with lumps, then add the salt and baking powder and whisk again.

Get your griddle pan nice and hot and wipe with some butter, so it's glistening but not wet.

Don't worry if you don't have a griddle pan; I love using mine because of the stripes it makes but you can use an ordinary small pancake or frying pan – as long as it is ovenproof. Pour in a tablespoon of batter and cook the griddle for about 1 minute, until bubbles start to form on the surface. Pop the pan on to the top shelf of your hot oven for 1 minute, until the griddle looks matt, rather than shiny. Remove from the oven and flip the griddle over with a spatula. Cook the other side on top of the stove for about 1 minute.

Repeat with the rest of your batter – you should get at least 10 griddles from this amount of batter but the quantities are easily halved and I often make up half the amount if it's just for the boys.

I always thought there was something vaguely mysterious about marzipan when I was little; that it was this wonderful sweetmeat that came from distant shores and only really featured when Santa was almost due. Megsie would stuff dates with it, or it would be hidden in the sugar-dusted hills of a stollen cake... I've since discovered you can make it yourself from three ingredients that are not very mysterious at all. JOY.

Marzipan

Prepare in 5 mins · Makes 225g

175g ground almonds
125g icing sugar
1 egg

Put the ground almonds and icing sugar into a large mixing bowl and stir together. Add the egg and keep stirring, although you will probably have to get your hands in the bowl and knead it to mix it properly. That's it – marzipan!

Wrap in cling film and keep in the fridge – ready for your next marzipan moment. I can recommend using it for Megsie's Dates. (Coming to a page near you soon...)

I never liked dates until I discovered Medjool dates, which taste like
I imagine amber would taste, should you be able to eat it. Granny Megsie
used to make these date sweets at Christmas and New Year and I
always wished I liked them, as I so loved the way they looked.
I like them now...

Megsie's Dates

Prepare in 10 mins · Cook in 5 mins · Makes 24

12 Medjool dates
6 walnuts or pecans
homemade marzipan (see page opposite)
200g caster sugar

Halve and de-stone your dates (you can do
this with your fingers as they are so lovely
and soft). Break each walnut or pecan
roughly into quarters.

Push a generous blob of marzipan inside
each date half and then press a piece of
walnut or pecan on top of the marzipan.

Make a caramel by placing the caster sugar
in a non-stick frying pan. Gently melt over
a low heat until it turns golden – don't stir,
just joggle it as it melts and take it off the
heat as soon as it reaches a golden colour.
Spoon over the top of your marzipan, date
and walnut creations. I do this on some
baking paper, so that when the caramel has
set they are easy to peel off.

Beautiful. A lovely present on a little plate.
Or, keep in an airtight container for up to
a week.

This is one of the first recipes I remember making, ever. Probably about the same time I invented 'Sophie Cake' (see 'Introduction')... My dad was directing Penelope Keith in an Alan Ayckbourn trilogy called *The Norman Conquests*. They were brilliant with a completely amazing cast. I was in awe of them all. I can't remember why, but Penelope Keith gave me this recipe. I still have the original recipe that I wrote down as a child with 'Penny Keef's Truffles' written at the top in coloured pencil. I'm not sure I added the rum then. These are a perfect wee Christmas pressie – just pop a few on a pretty saucer and wrap them in cellophane. Thank you to the inimitable Ms P. Keith and hats off to the entire company of *The Norman Conquests* circa 1974 – you were an utter inspiration to a little me, and continue to be so.

Penny's Truffles

Prepare in 10 mins · Cook in 5 mins · Makes about 35

200g digestive biscuits
200g dark chocolate
100g butter, diced
4 tbsp double cream
5 tbsp ground almonds
2 tbsp rum
4 tsp icing sugar
3 tbsp cocoa powder
2 tbsp chocolate vermicelli

First put your digestive biscuits into a plastic bag and bash with a rolling pin until you have fine crumbs. Set aside.

Melt the chocolate in a bain-marie: break it into pieces and place in a heatproof bowl set over a pan of just-simmering water. When the chocolate has melted add the diced butter and stir until it melts into the chocolate. Remove from the heat.

Add it to the cream, digestive crumbs, ground almonds, rum, icing sugar and 2 tablespoons of the cocoa powder. Stir until well combined then cover and chill in the fridge for at least half an hour.

Mix the remaining tablespoon of cocoa powder with the vermicelli and tip on to a plate. Use a teaspoon to scoop out the truffle mixture and roll between your palms to make a round ball. Roll each ball in the vermicelli/cocoa mix until covered and arrange on a pretty plate.

Thankyoooous!

For the team that is Faber I offer up an outsized amount of grateful thanks. I managed to get through their door one morning in my pyjamas (cunningly disguised as daywear, I might add) with a children's story under one arm and the possibility (they spotted and I didn't) of something from a medium oven under the other. Far from throwing me out on my ear they welcomed me in and put the kettle on. It's been a blast so far and I'm looking forward to the next course! They are such a bunch of clever, clever peeps – I can only hope some of it rubs off (spelling at the very least). So ALL my caps doffed to those at Faber:

The self-raising flower, Leah Thaxton.
The binding eggs and whisk, Alice Swan.
The sugar-sweet dusting of Emma Eldridge.
The hot and cold beverageness of Grace 'Slippers' Gleave.
The no-nonsense ashettes of Anna Pallai and Hannah Love.
The serviettes of Susan Holmes and John Grindrod.

In the larder beyond Great Russell Street are revealed:
Bren Parkins-Knight with the ever-on oven, making sense of it all – thank you.
Friederike Huber being ridiculously arty – thank you.
Clare Sayer telling it how it is – thank you.
Annie Lee proofing the pudding – thank you.
Lydia Brun footling through cupboards and saying 'This'll work!' – thank you.
Al Richardson for turning up with his kitchen table (literally) and two awesome eyes – thank you.
Frankie Unsworth for being absurdly calm and brilliant – thank you.
Katy McPhee for being my amazing aproned friend-on-the-bend – thank you.

I would also like to extend my humongous admiring thanks to:
Lauren Pearson, my beautiful agent at Curtis Brown for taking an untested recipe called 'me' on and for being utterly fab.

The awesome triumvirate that is Claire Maroussas, Anna Tune and Clarence Conway at Independent Talent for supporting this particular turn on every turn.

Furthermore, thanks with lashings of gravy to:
Tony, Effie, Chris, Mike, Kim and Helen at 'Tony's Continental'
Maurizio and the gals at 'Amici' Deli
Pete and Paul at 'Scott's of East Finchley'
Dave, Gary, Big Bob, Al and all the lads at 'Midhurst Butchers'
Keith, Gabby, Ray and the team at 'Amy's Hardware', East Finchley
Megan and Ruth at 'Cha Cha Cha' of Muswell Hill Mews
Dan and Martha at 'Franco's'
Sandra Mattocks and the 'Crisis' café
Edith Crack and the 'Casserole Club'

A very special and particularly well seasoned thank you must got to the *MasterChef* team, without whom... Particularly John T and Gregg W, Sue Green, Karen and Karim, Lucy, Molly, Charlotte, Bev (at Plank PR) and ALL on the floor. Plus the inimitable 'Team 3': Russell Grant, Todd Carty, Jodie Kidd and Susannah Constantine – also Charley 'Papaya' Boorman.

And all my inestimable and vividly inspiring family and pals who have contributed and let me use and abuse their recipes.

The utterly colossal cherry plus multi-coloured sprinkles of thanks must go to (the official tasters) Richard and our boys, Ernie and Walter: the gravy in my boat... Well, the boat, the oars and the sea, and the land in sight... and the flittery flag and the lights, and the toots of the horn and the calm and the storm and the salt and the spume... am I taking this analogy too far?

'A Good Year for Plums' by Soph T. by kind permission of Charlie Palmer and Claire Skinner
'Tart' By Soph T. by kind permission of Tamsin Olivier
'Tony's Carrots' by Soph T. by kind permission of Julian Simpson

Last day of the shoot

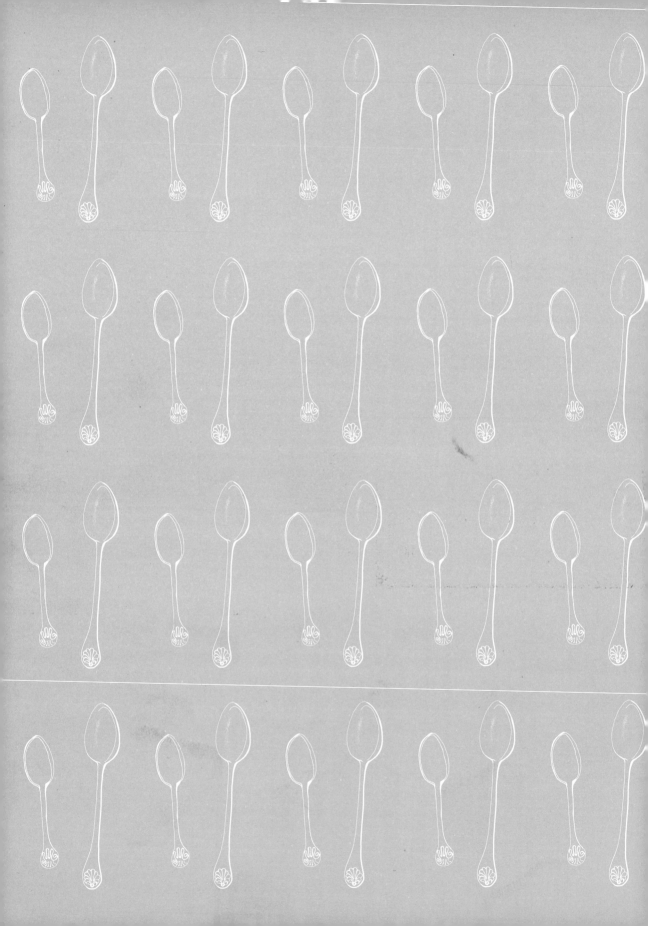